# MESSAGES
## FROM THE
# Fairies
## COLORING BOOK

# MESSAGES
## FROM THE
# *Fairies*
### COLORING BOOK

## DOREEN VIRTUE

Illustrations by Norma J. Burnell

**HAY HOUSE**

Carlsbad, California • New York • London • Sydney
Johannesburg • Vancouver • New Delhi

*Published and distributed in the United States by:* Hay House, Inc.: www.hayhouse
.com® • *Published and distributed in Australia by:* Hay House Australia Pty. Ltd.: www
.hayhouse.com.au • *Published and distributed in the United Kingdom by:* Hay House
UK, Ltd.: www.hayhouse.co.uk • *Published and distributed in the Republic of South
Africa by:* Hay House SA (Pty), Ltd.: www.hayhouse.co.za • *Distributed in Canada by:*
Raincoast Books: www.raincoast.com • *Published in India by*: Hay House Publishers
India: www.hayhouse.co.in

*Cover and interior design:* Leanne Siu Anastasi
*Cover and interior illustrations:* Norma J. Burnell

**Tradepaper ISBN:** 978-1-4019-5202-0

10  9  8  7  6  5  4  3  2  1
1st edition, July 2016
Printed in the United States of America

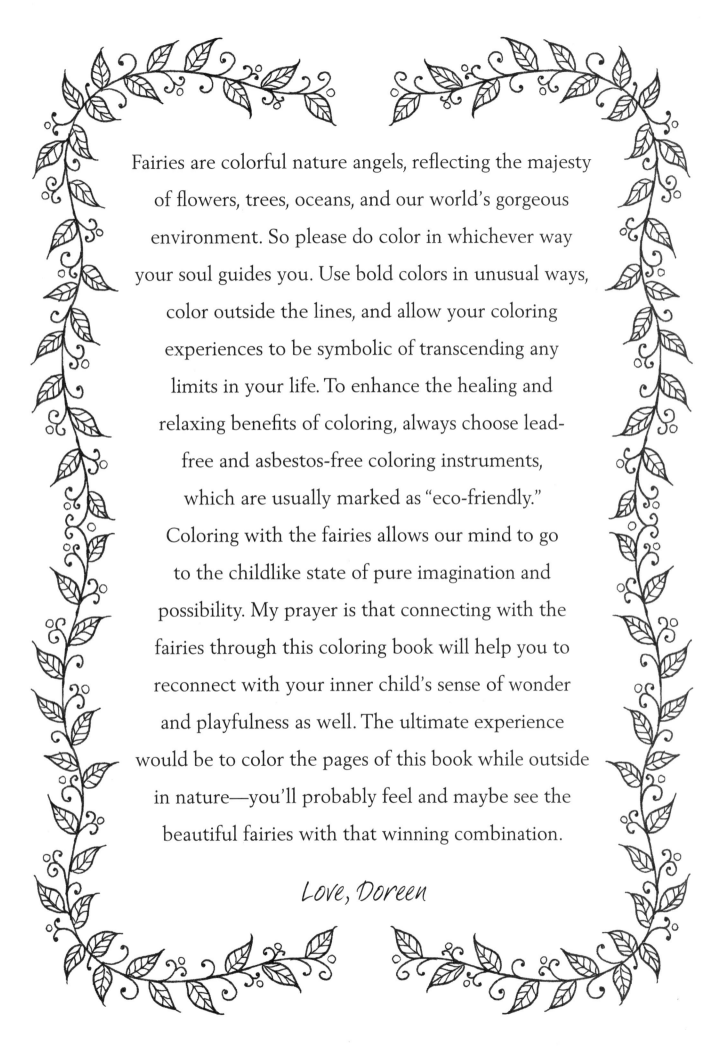

Fairies are colorful nature angels, reflecting the majesty of flowers, trees, oceans, and our world's gorgeous environment. So please do color in whichever way your soul guides you. Use bold colors in unusual ways, color outside the lines, and allow your coloring experiences to be symbolic of transcending any limits in your life. To enhance the healing and relaxing benefits of coloring, always choose lead-free and asbestos-free coloring instruments, which are usually marked as "eco-friendly." Coloring with the fairies allows our mind to go to the childlike state of pure imagination and possibility. My prayer is that connecting with the fairies through this coloring book will help you to reconnect with your inner child's sense of wonder and playfulness as well. The ultimate experience would be to color the pages of this book while outside in nature—you'll probably feel and maybe see the beautiful fairies with that winning combination.

*Love, Doreen*

Hello, we are the fairies who are sometimes
called the "angels of nature," because
it's our job to watch over the land,
plants, trees, flowers, water, air, and all
of the animals and birds of our planet.
We love the Earth, and are working
hard to keep it healthy and clean —and
we appreciate your help with this!

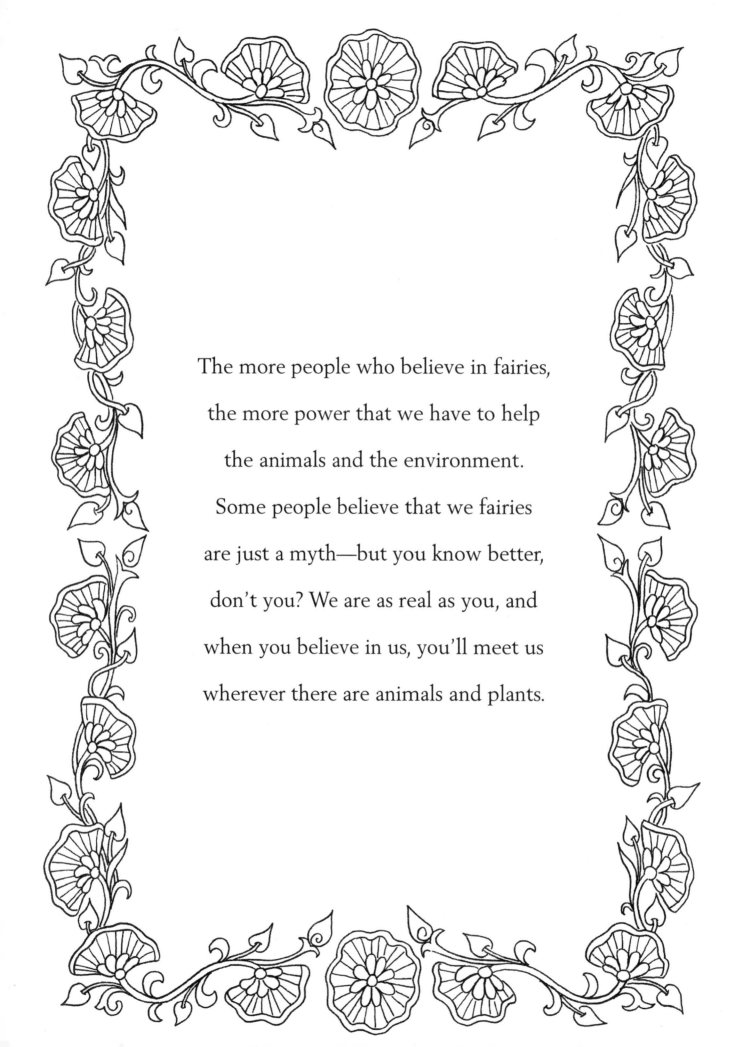

The more people who believe in fairies,

the more power that we have to help

the animals and the environment.

Some people believe that we fairies

are just a myth—but you know better,

don't you? We are as real as you, and

when you believe in us, you'll meet us

wherever there are animals and plants.

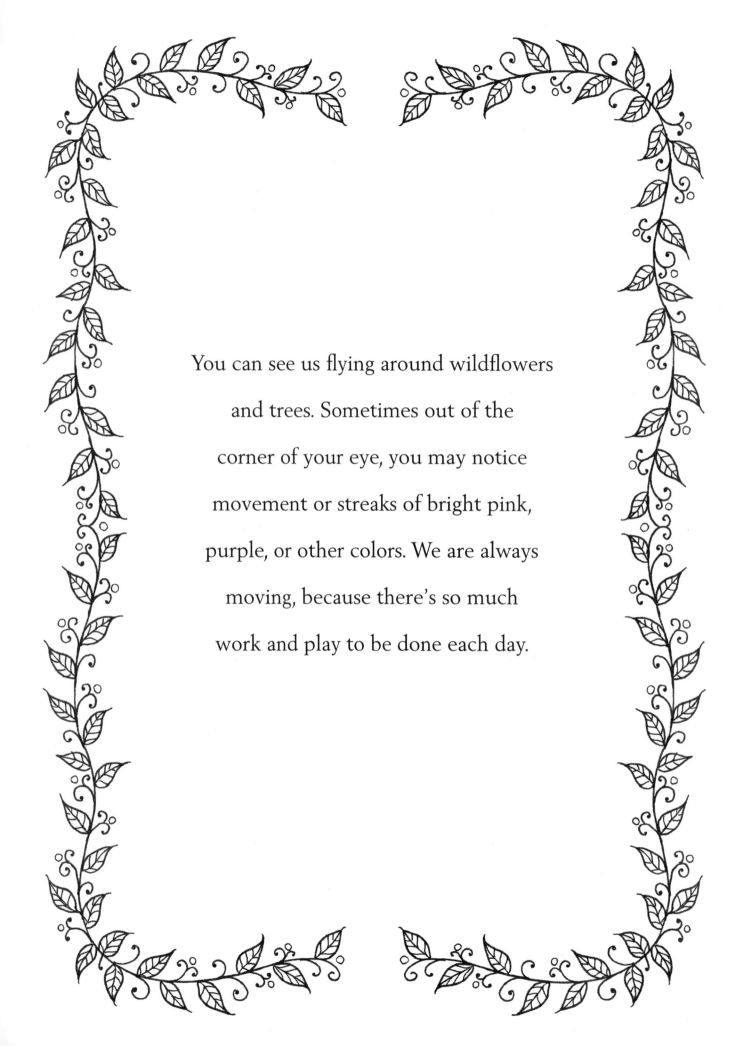

You can see us flying around wildflowers and trees. Sometimes out of the corner of your eye, you may notice movement or streaks of bright pink, purple, or other colors. We are always moving, because there's so much work and play to be done each day.

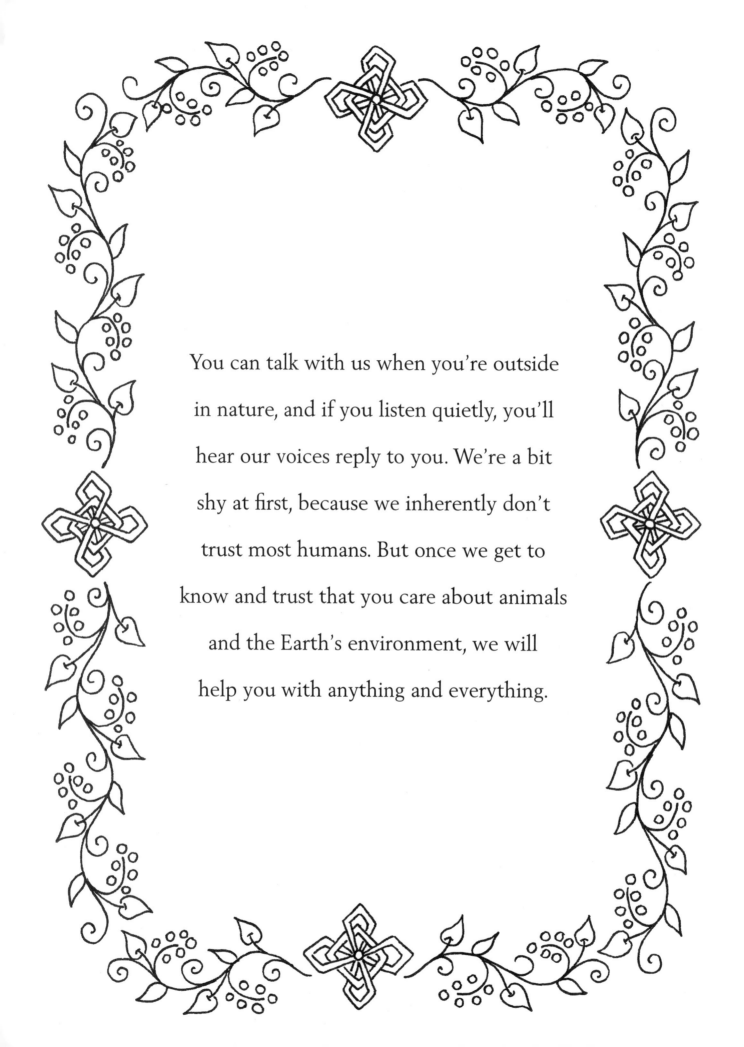

You can talk with us when you're outside in nature, and if you listen quietly, you'll hear our voices reply to you. We're a bit shy at first, because we inherently don't trust most humans. But once we get to know and trust that you care about animals and the Earth's environment, we will help you with anything and everything.

We can teach you how to make your
wishes come true, by holding a vision in
your mind of your desire already being real
right now. Once you hold this vision, let
your heart get happy about this thought.
The more happiness you have about your
dream being a current reality, the faster
the vision crystallizes into form for you.

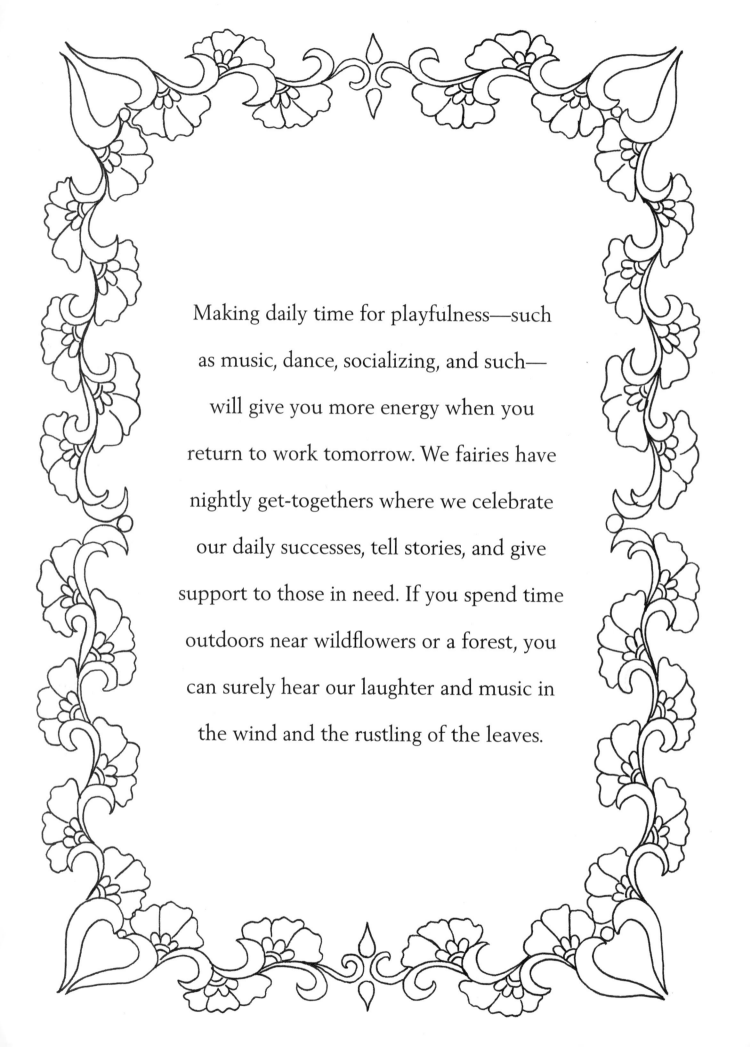

Making daily time for playfulness—such as music, dance, socializing, and such—will give you more energy when you return to work tomorrow. We fairies have nightly get-togethers where we celebrate our daily successes, tell stories, and give support to those in need. If you spend time outdoors near wildflowers or a forest, you can surely hear our laughter and music in the wind and the rustling of the leaves.

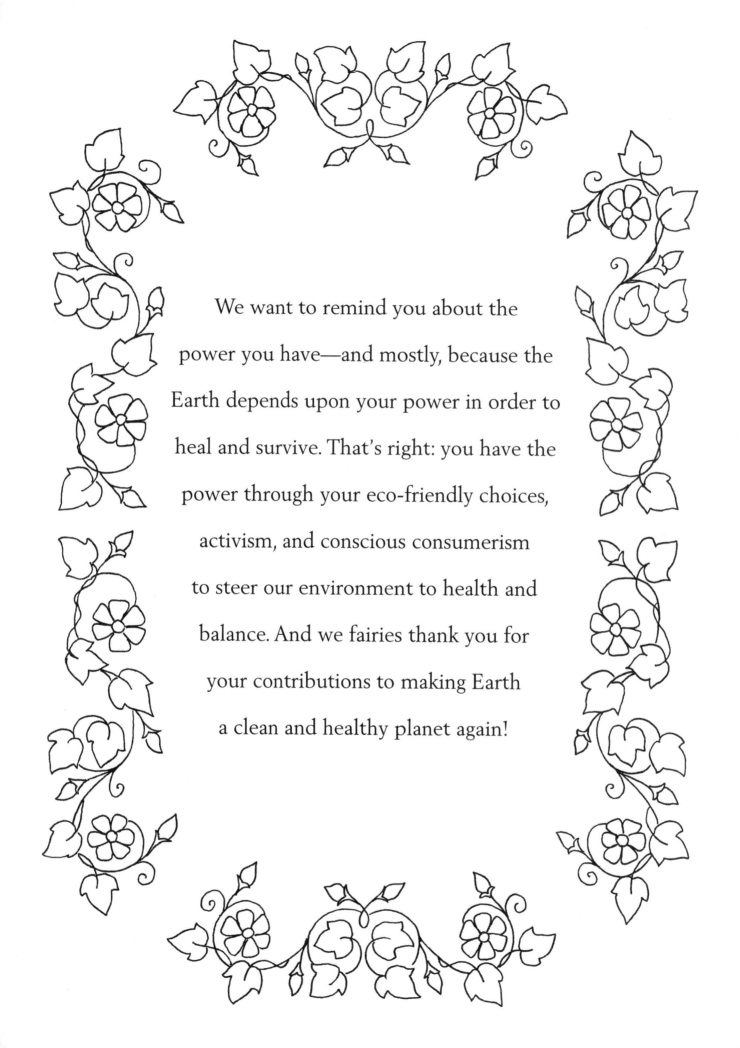

We want to remind you about the

power you have—and mostly, because the

Earth depends upon your power in order to

heal and survive. That's right: you have the

power through your eco-friendly choices,

activism, and conscious consumerism

to steer our environment to health and

balance. And we fairies thank you for

your contributions to making Earth

a clean and healthy planet again!

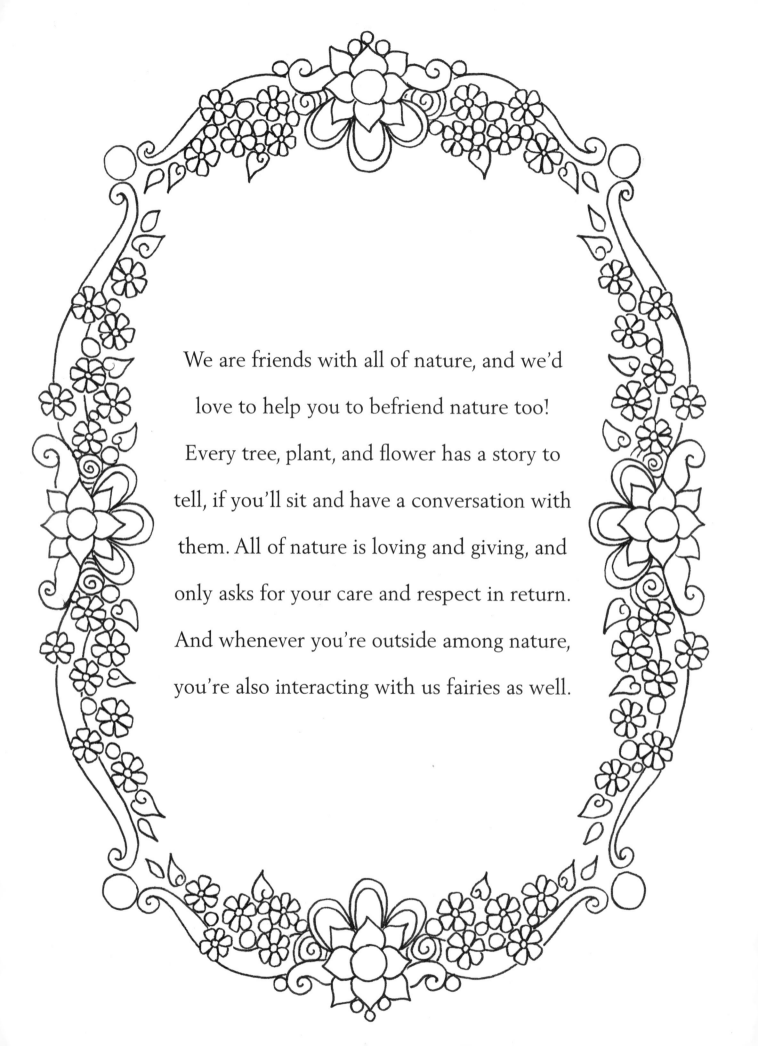

We are friends with all of nature, and we'd
love to help you to befriend nature too!
Every tree, plant, and flower has a story to
tell, if you'll sit and have a conversation with
them. All of nature is loving and giving, and
only asks for your care and respect in return.
And whenever you're outside among nature,
you're also interacting with us fairies as well.

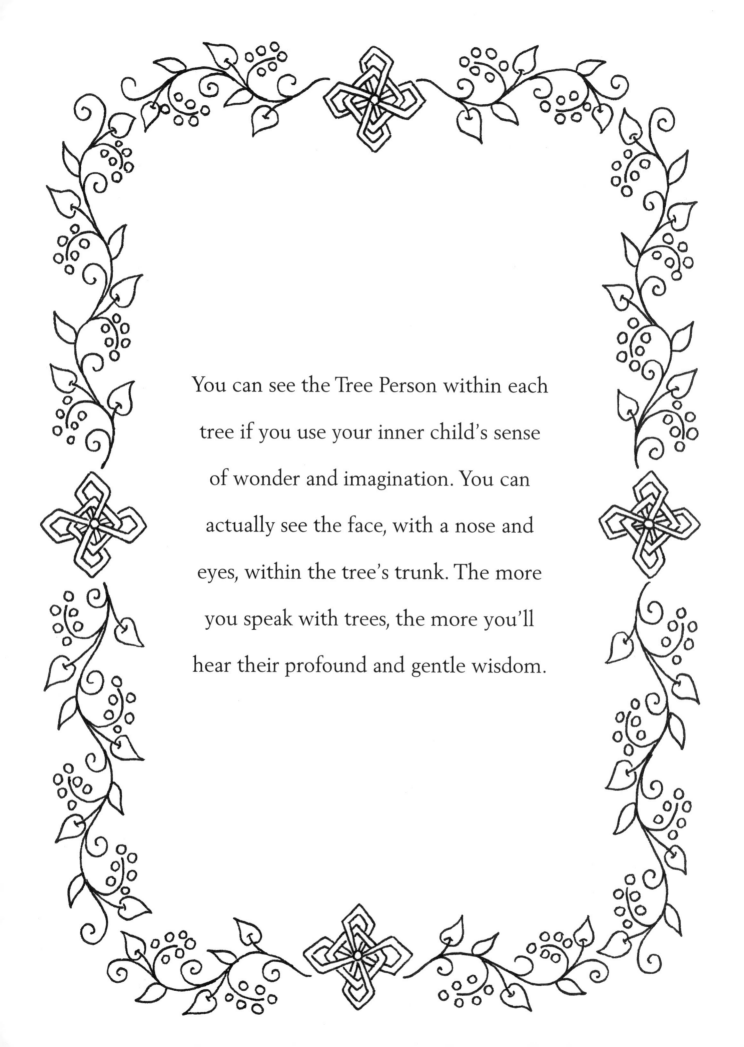

You can see the Tree Person within each tree if you use your inner child's sense of wonder and imagination. You can actually see the face, with a nose and eyes, within the tree's trunk. The more you speak with trees, the more you'll hear their profound and gentle wisdom.

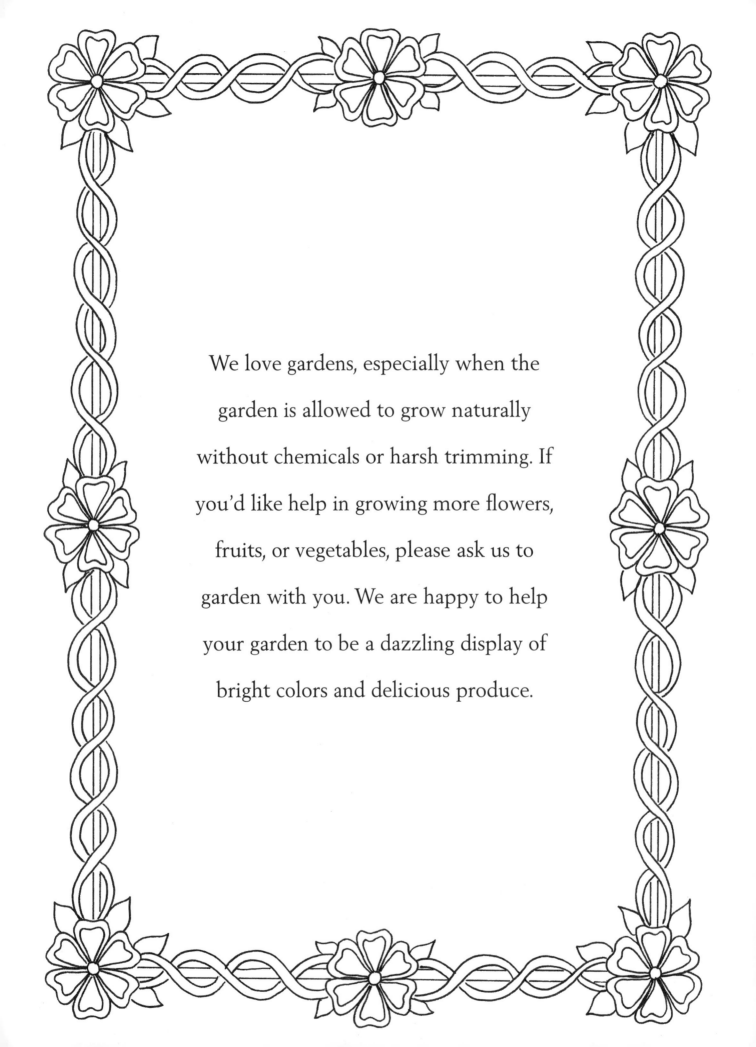

We love gardens, especially when the garden is allowed to grow naturally without chemicals or harsh trimming. If you'd like help in growing more flowers, fruits, or vegetables, please ask us to garden with you. We are happy to help your garden to be a dazzling display of bright colors and delicious produce.

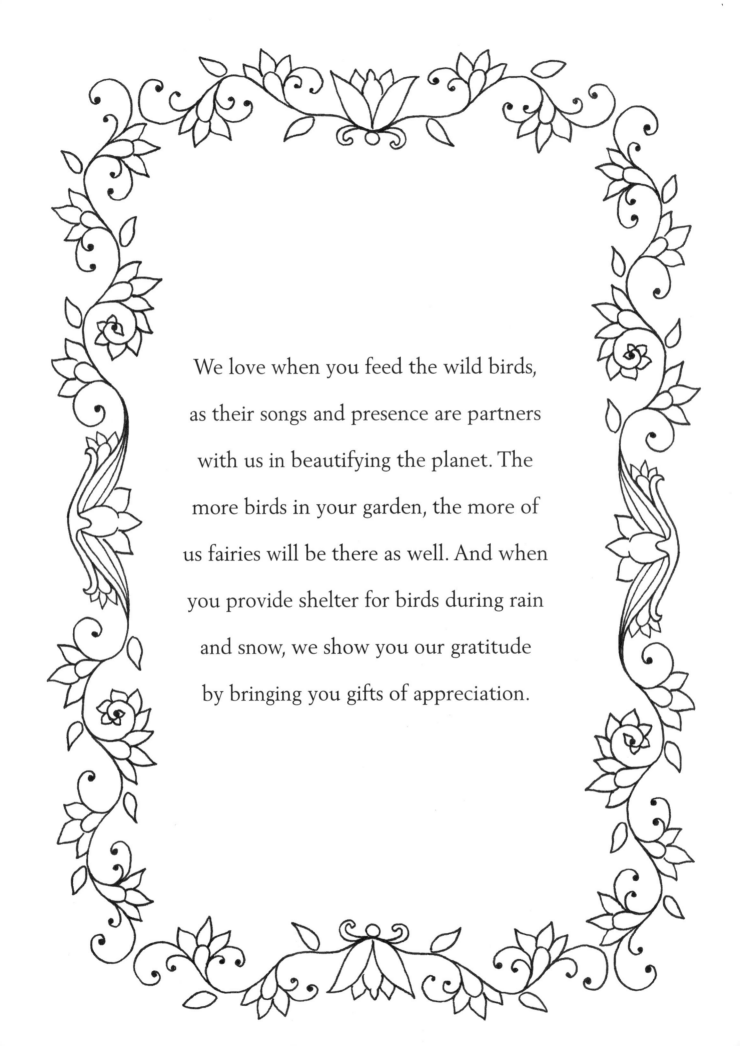

We love when you feed the wild birds,
as their songs and presence are partners
with us in beautifying the planet. The
more birds in your garden, the more of
us fairies will be there as well. And when
you provide shelter for birds during rain
and snow, we show you our gratitude
by bringing you gifts of appreciation.

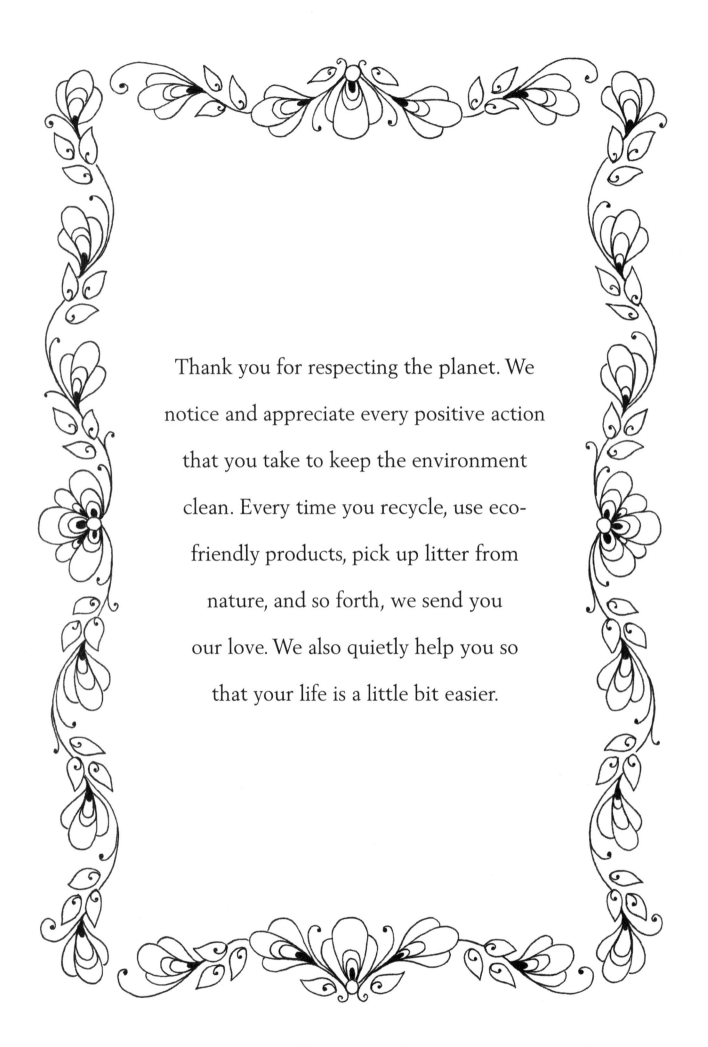

Thank you for respecting the planet. We notice and appreciate every positive action that you take to keep the environment clean. Every time you recycle, use eco-friendly products, pick up litter from nature, and so forth, we send you our love. We also quietly help you so that your life is a little bit easier.

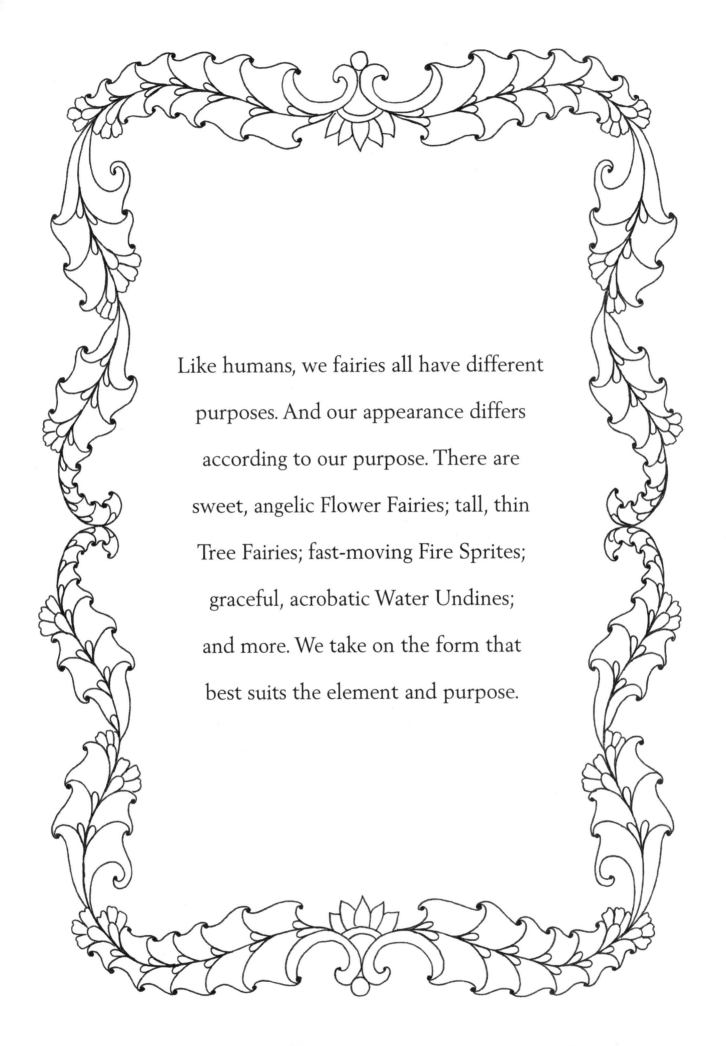

Like humans, we fairies all have different

purposes. And our appearance differs

according to our purpose. There are

sweet, angelic Flower Fairies; tall, thin

Tree Fairies; fast-moving Fire Sprites;

graceful, acrobatic Water Undines;

and more. We take on the form that

best suits the element and purpose.

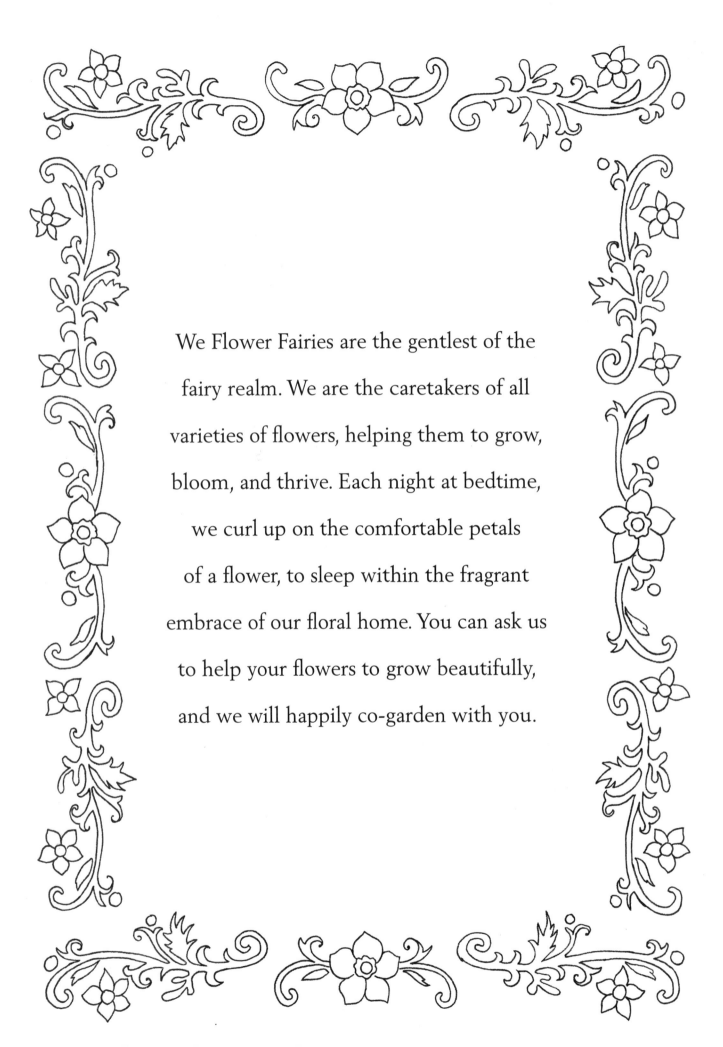

We Flower Fairies are the gentlest of the fairy realm. We are the caretakers of all varieties of flowers, helping them to grow, bloom, and thrive. Each night at bedtime, we curl up on the comfortable petals of a flower, to sleep within the fragrant embrace of our floral home. You can ask us to help your flowers to grow beautifully, and we will happily co-garden with you.

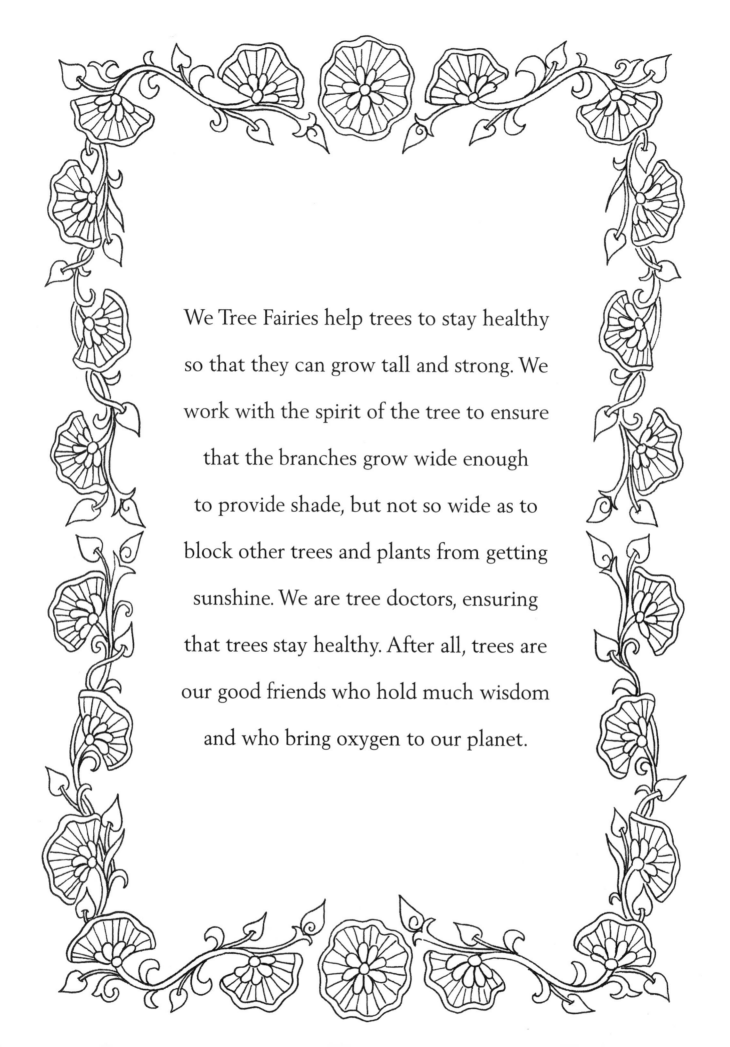

We Tree Fairies help trees to stay healthy
so that they can grow tall and strong. We
work with the spirit of the tree to ensure
that the branches grow wide enough
to provide shade, but not so wide as to
block other trees and plants from getting
sunshine. We are tree doctors, ensuring
that trees stay healthy. After all, trees are
our good friends who hold much wisdom
and who bring oxygen to our planet.

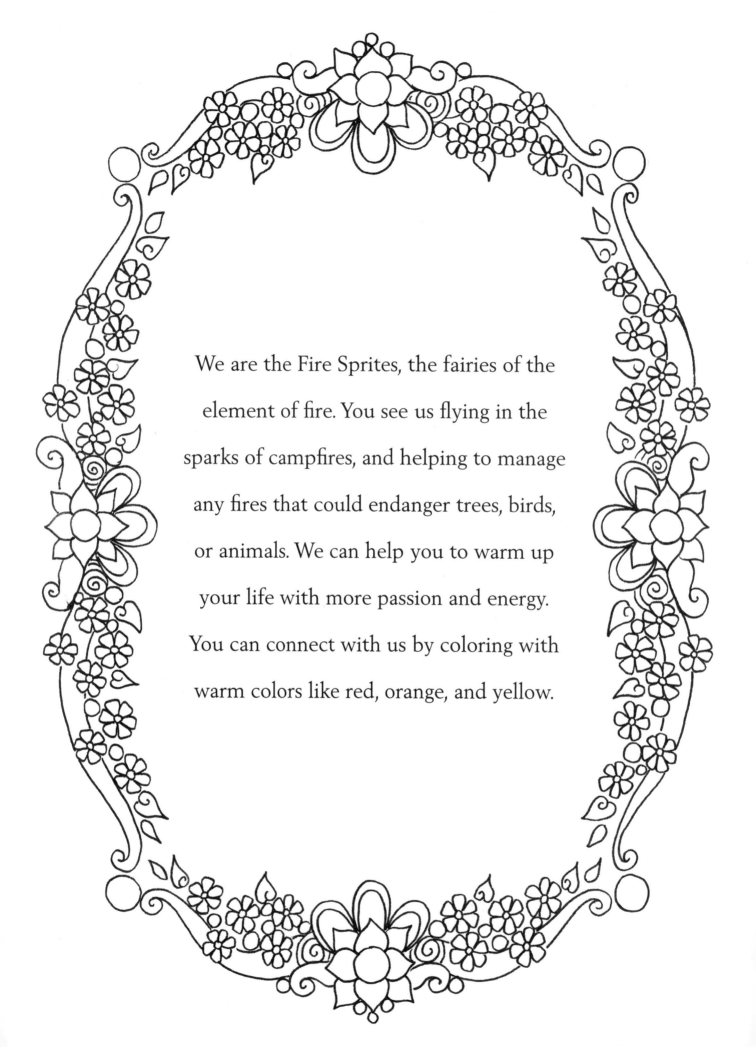

We are the Fire Sprites, the fairies of the element of fire. You see us flying in the sparks of campfires, and helping to manage any fires that could endanger trees, birds, or animals. We can help you to warm up your life with more passion and energy. You can connect with us by coloring with warm colors like red, orange, and yellow.

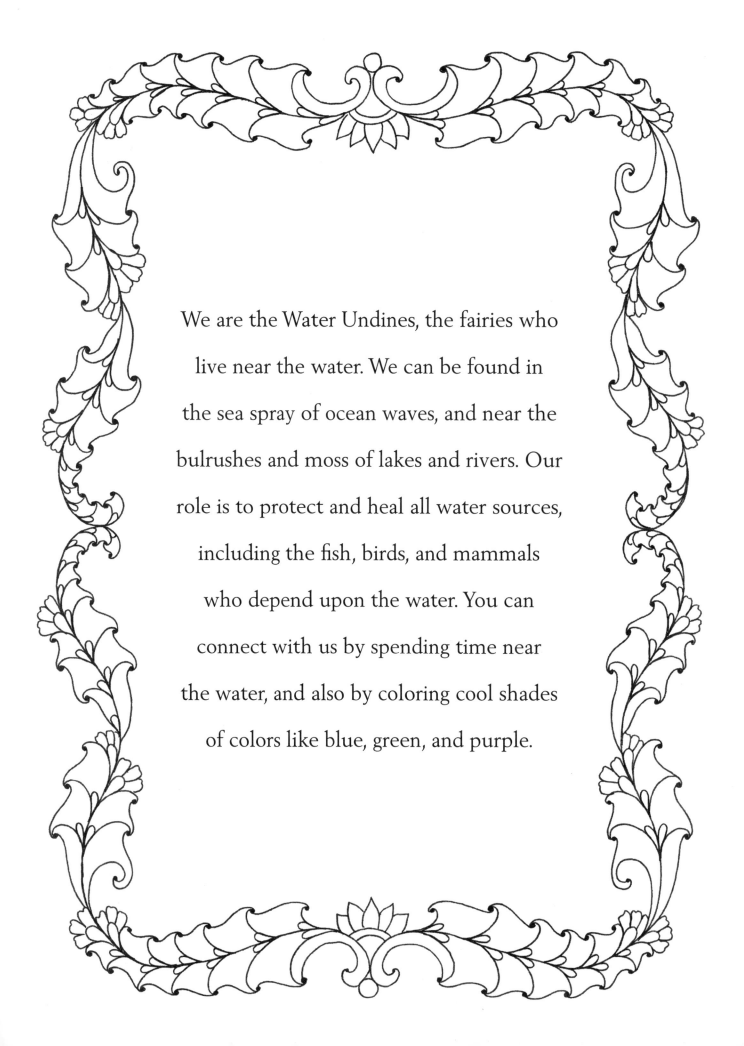

We are the Water Undines, the fairies who live near the water. We can be found in the sea spray of ocean waves, and near the bulrushes and moss of lakes and rivers. Our role is to protect and heal all water sources, including the fish, birds, and mammals who depend upon the water. You can connect with us by spending time near the water, and also by coloring cool shades of colors like blue, green, and purple.

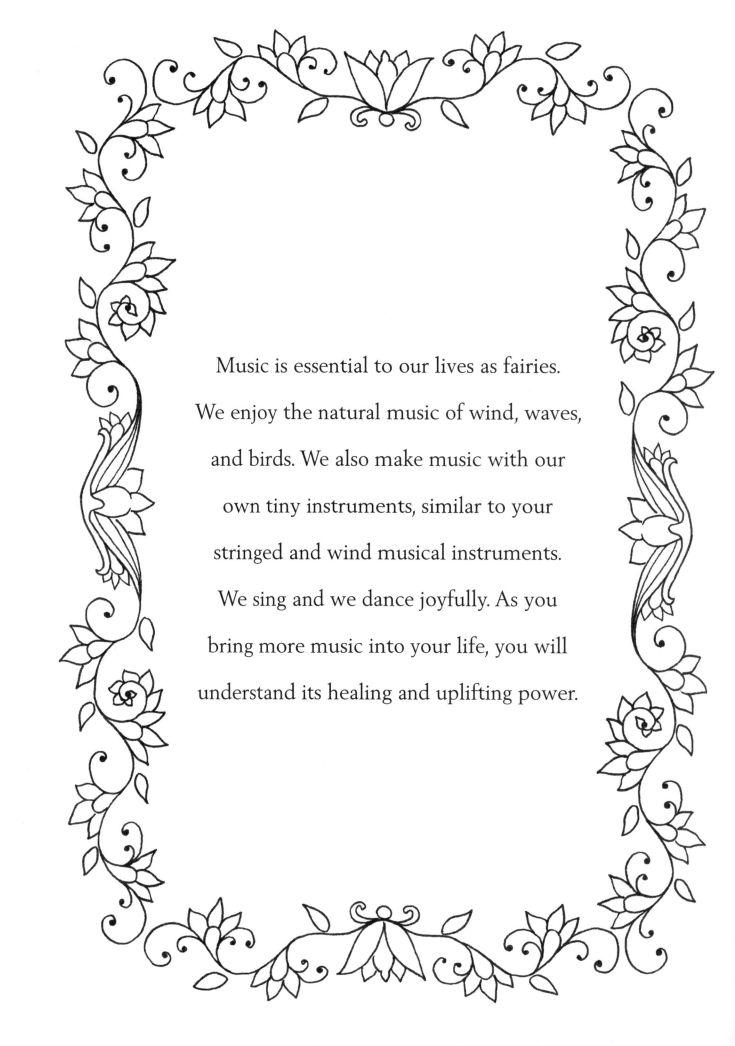

Music is essential to our lives as fairies.
We enjoy the natural music of wind, waves,
and birds. We also make music with our
own tiny instruments, similar to your
stringed and wind musical instruments.
We sing and we dance joyfully. As you
bring more music into your life, you will
understand its healing and uplifting power.

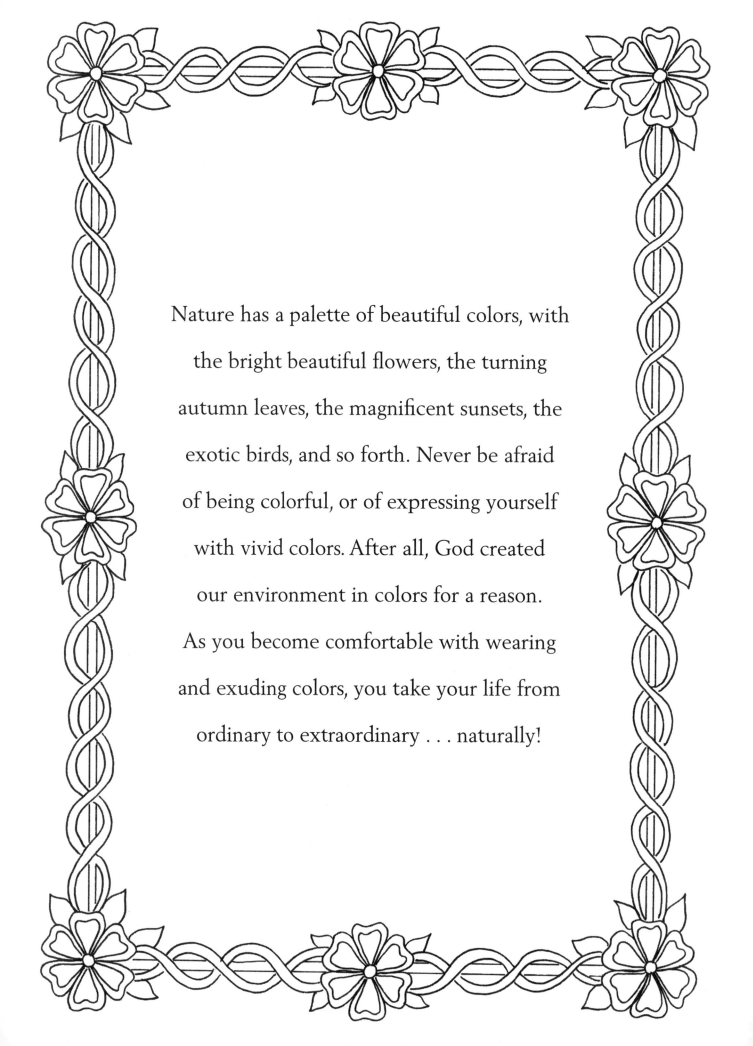

Nature has a palette of beautiful colors, with
the bright beautiful flowers, the turning
autumn leaves, the magnificent sunsets, the
exotic birds, and so forth. Never be afraid
of being colorful, or of expressing yourself
with vivid colors. After all, God created
our environment in colors for a reason.
As you become comfortable with wearing
and exuding colors, you take your life from
ordinary to extraordinary . . . naturally!

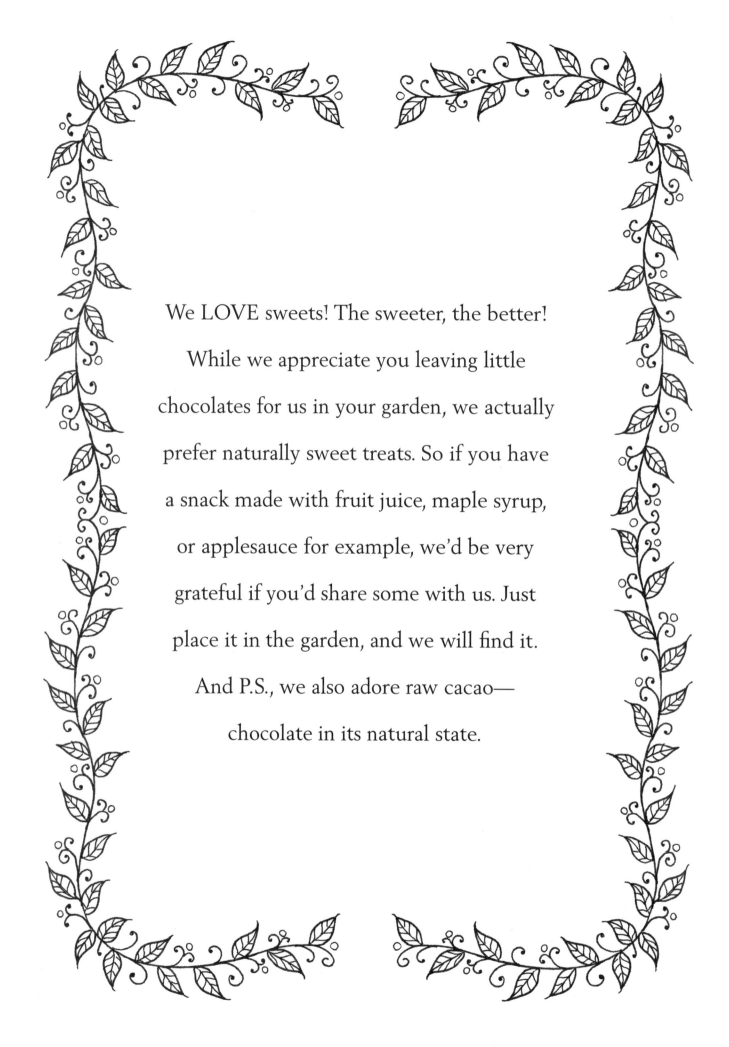

We LOVE sweets! The sweeter, the better!

While we appreciate you leaving little

chocolates for us in your garden, we actually

prefer naturally sweet treats. So if you have

a snack made with fruit juice, maple syrup,

or applesauce for example, we'd be very

grateful if you'd share some with us. Just

place it in the garden, and we will find it.

And P.S., we also adore raw cacao—

chocolate in its natural state.

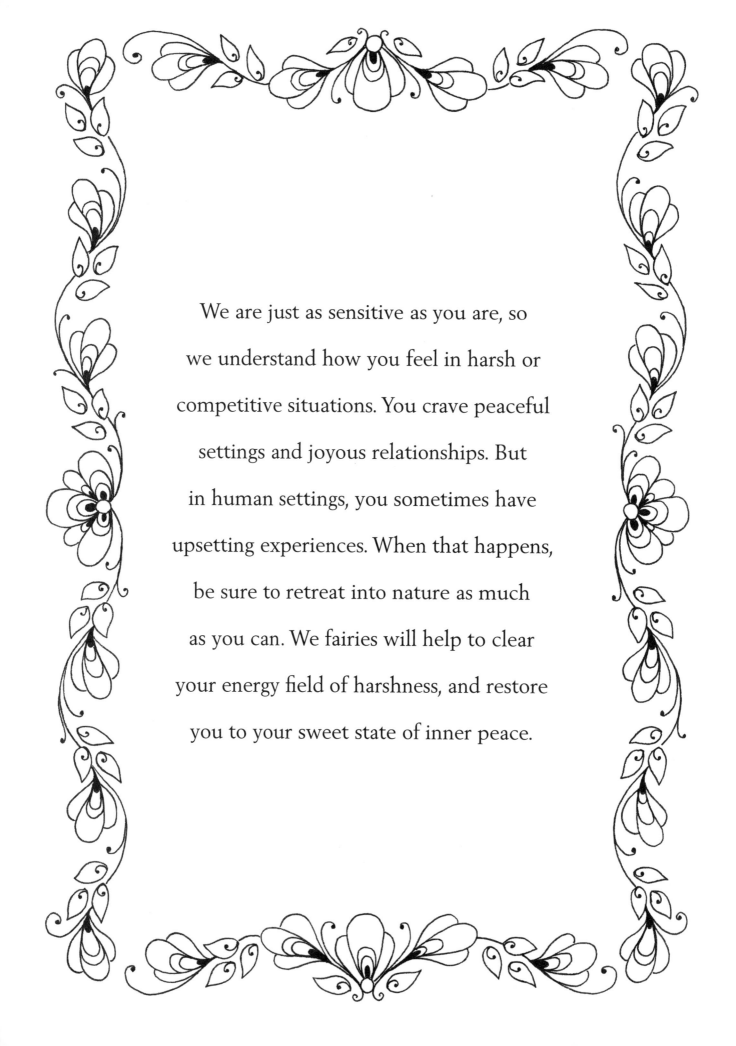

We are just as sensitive as you are, so
we understand how you feel in harsh or
competitive situations. You crave peaceful
settings and joyous relationships. But
in human settings, you sometimes have
upsetting experiences. When that happens,
be sure to retreat into nature as much
as you can. We fairies will help to clear
your energy field of harshness, and restore
you to your sweet state of inner peace.

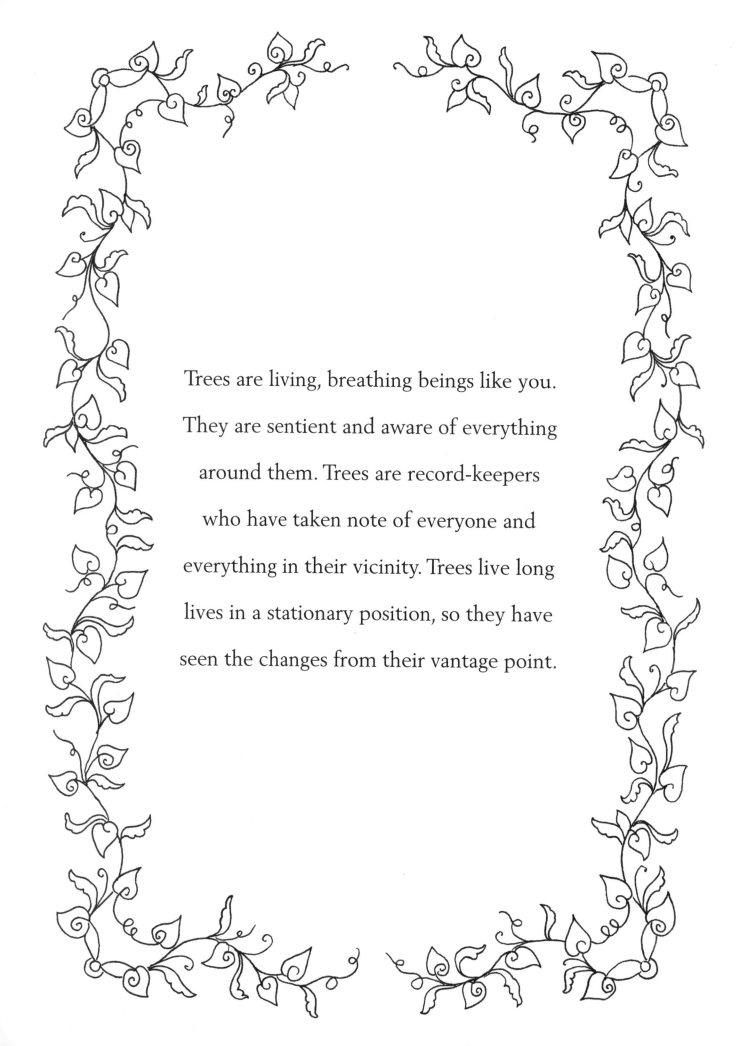

Trees are living, breathing beings like you.
They are sentient and aware of everything
around them. Trees are record-keepers
who have taken note of everyone and
everything in their vicinity. Trees live long
lives in a stationary position, so they have
seen the changes from their vantage point.

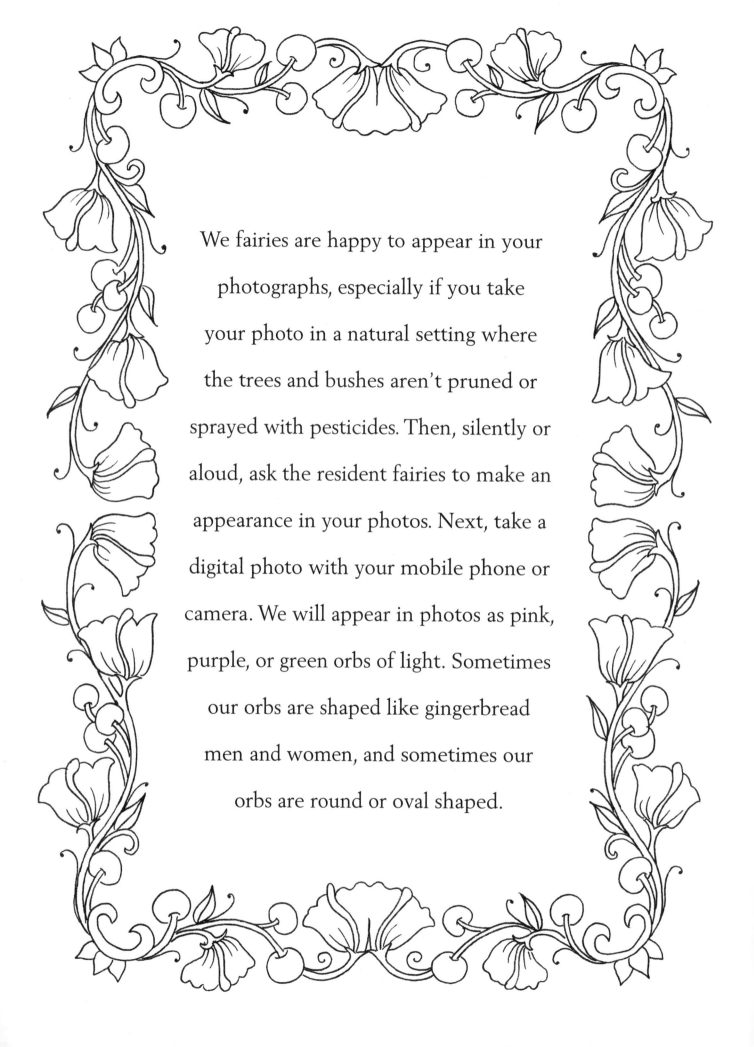

We fairies are happy to appear in your photographs, especially if you take your photo in a natural setting where the trees and bushes aren't pruned or sprayed with pesticides. Then, silently or aloud, ask the resident fairies to make an appearance in your photos. Next, take a digital photo with your mobile phone or camera. We will appear in photos as pink, purple, or green orbs of light. Sometimes our orbs are shaped like gingerbread men and women, and sometimes our orbs are round or oval shaped.

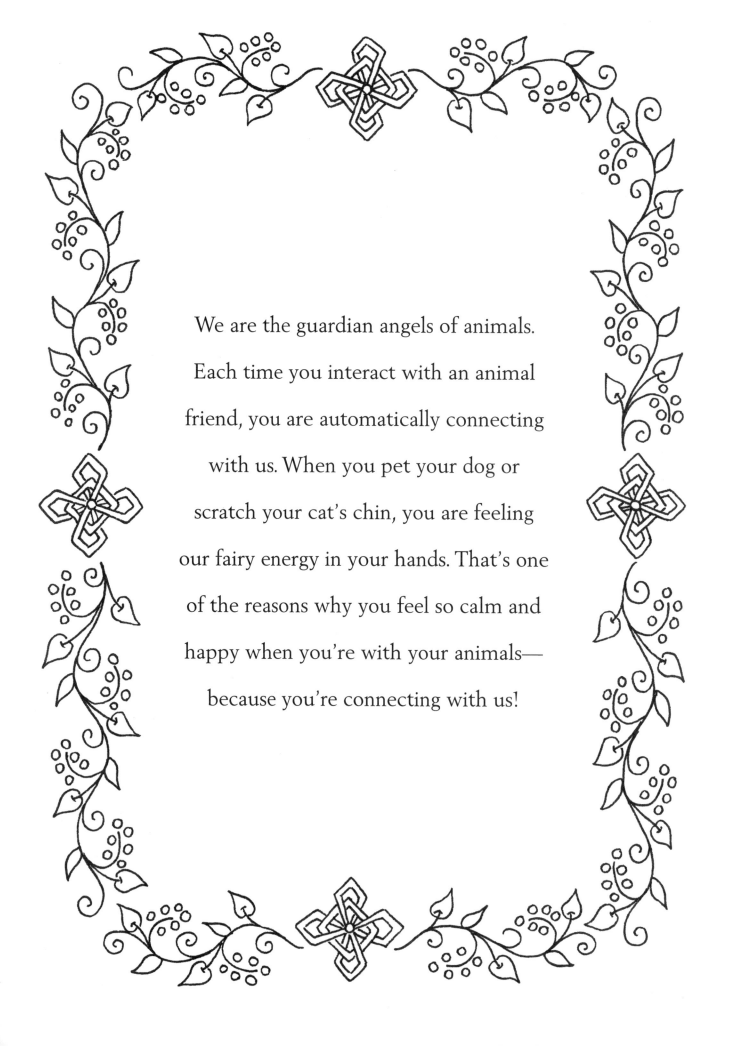

We are the guardian angels of animals.
Each time you interact with an animal
friend, you are automatically connecting
with us. When you pet your dog or
scratch your cat's chin, you are feeling
our fairy energy in your hands. That's one
of the reasons why you feel so calm and
happy when you're with your animals—
because you're connecting with us!

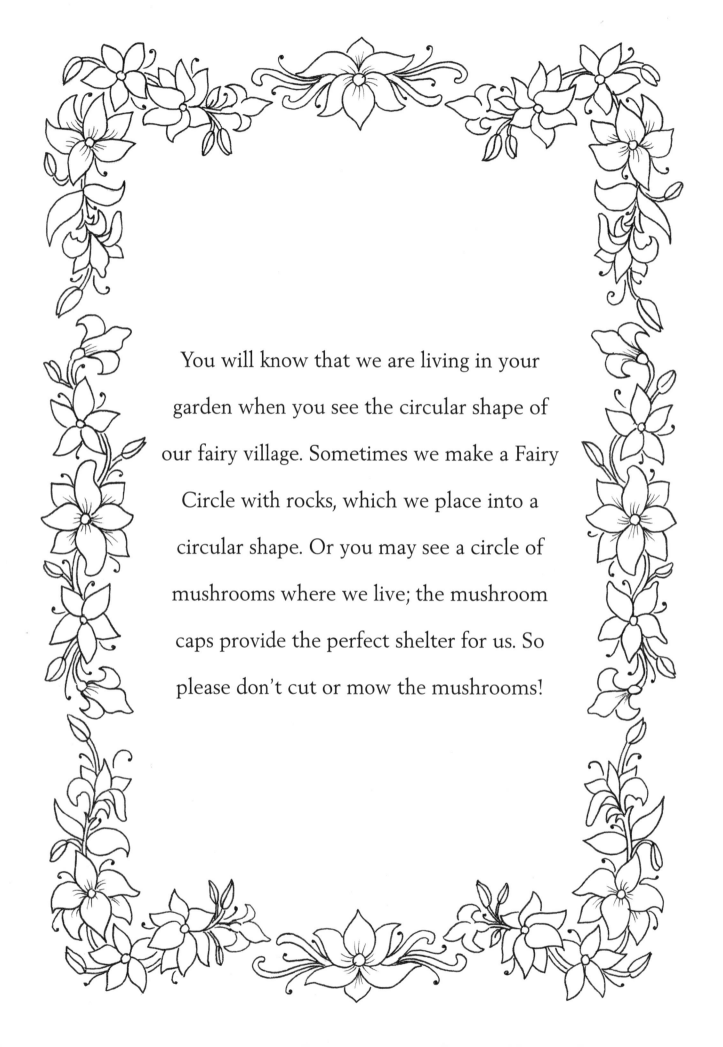

You will know that we are living in your garden when you see the circular shape of our fairy village. Sometimes we make a Fairy Circle with rocks, which we place into a circular shape. Or you may see a circle of mushrooms where we live; the mushroom caps provide the perfect shelter for us. So please don't cut or mow the mushrooms!

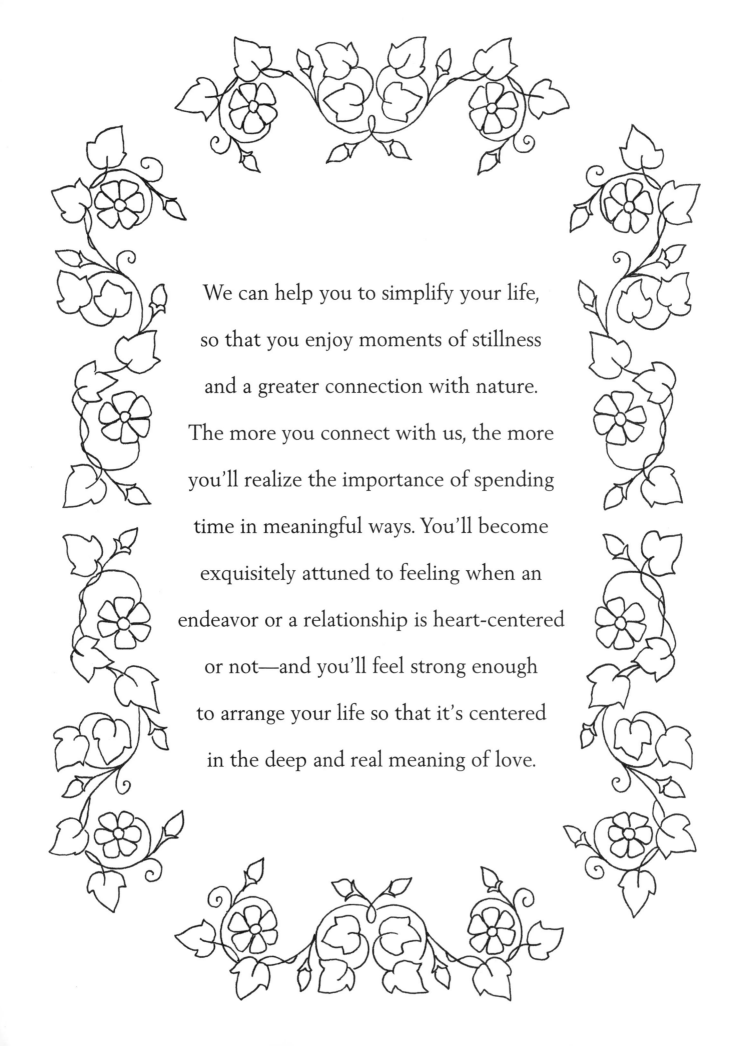

We can help you to simplify your life,

so that you enjoy moments of stillness

and a greater connection with nature.

The more you connect with us, the more

you'll realize the importance of spending

time in meaningful ways. You'll become

exquisitely attuned to feeling when an

endeavor or a relationship is heart-centered

or not—and you'll feel strong enough

to arrange your life so that it's centered

in the deep and real meaning of love.

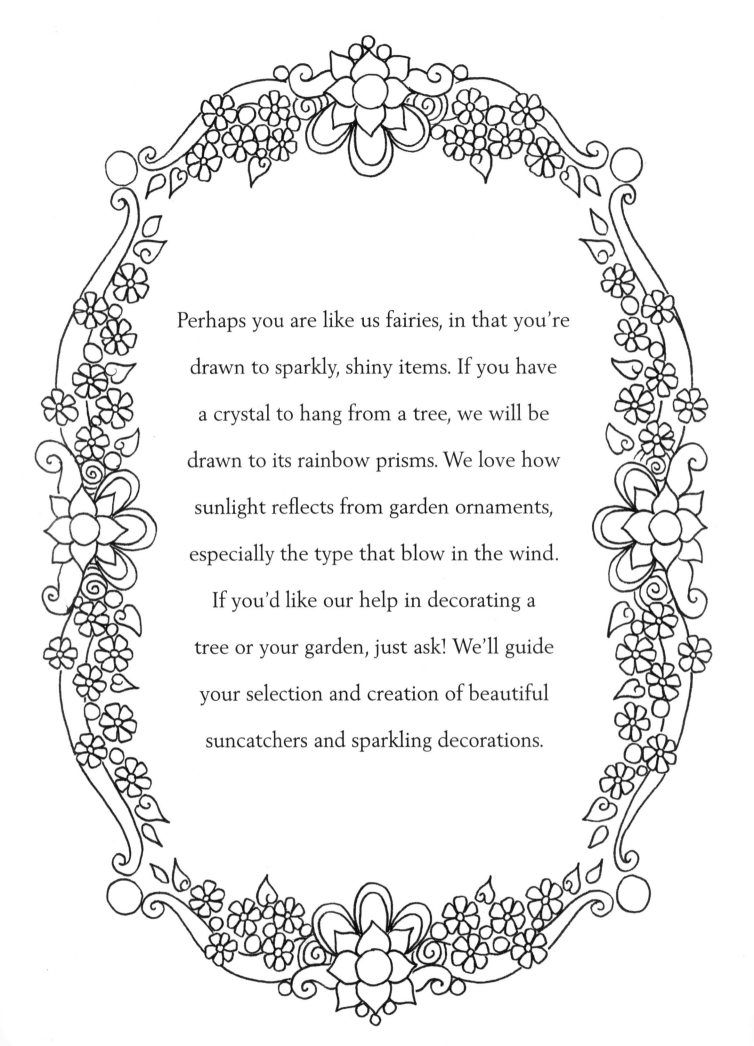

Perhaps you are like us fairies, in that you're drawn to sparkly, shiny items. If you have a crystal to hang from a tree, we will be drawn to its rainbow prisms. We love how sunlight reflects from garden ornaments, especially the type that blow in the wind. If you'd like our help in decorating a tree or your garden, just ask! We'll guide your selection and creation of beautiful suncatchers and sparkling decorations.

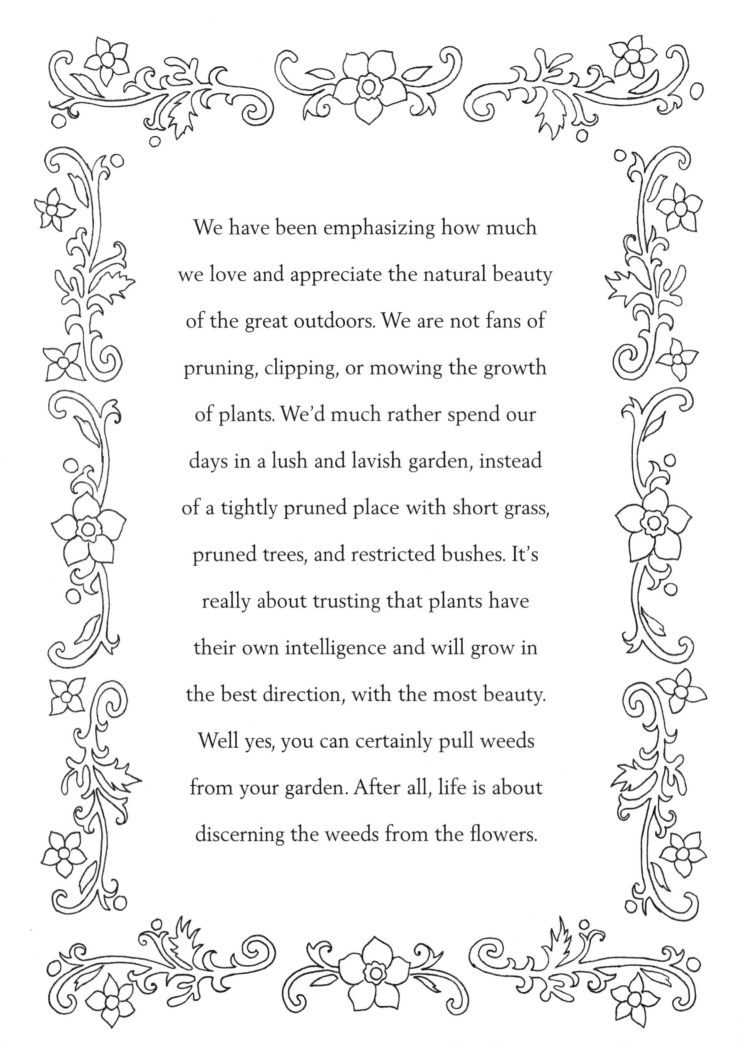

We have been emphasizing how much
we love and appreciate the natural beauty
of the great outdoors. We are not fans of
pruning, clipping, or mowing the growth
of plants. We'd much rather spend our
days in a lush and lavish garden, instead
of a tightly pruned place with short grass,
pruned trees, and restricted bushes. It's
really about trusting that plants have
their own intelligence and will grow in
the best direction, with the most beauty.
Well yes, you can certainly pull weeds
from your garden. After all, life is about
discerning the weeds from the flowers.

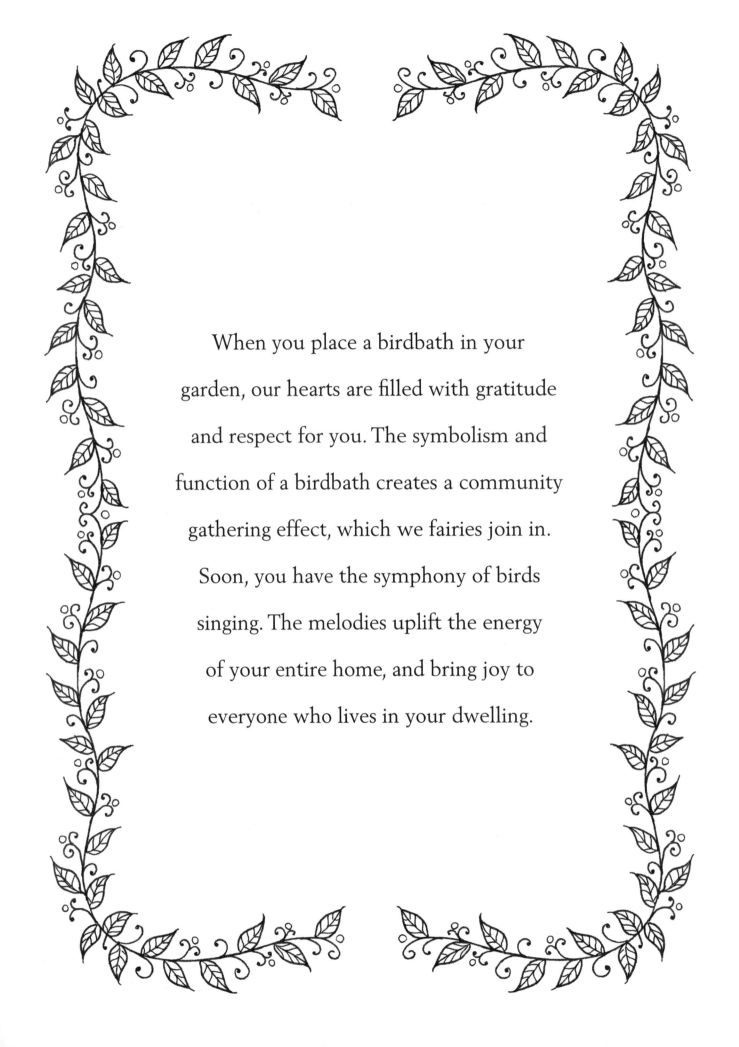

When you place a birdbath in your garden, our hearts are filled with gratitude and respect for you. The symbolism and function of a birdbath creates a community gathering effect, which we fairies join in. Soon, you have the symphony of birds singing. The melodies uplift the energy of your entire home, and bring joy to everyone who lives in your dwelling.

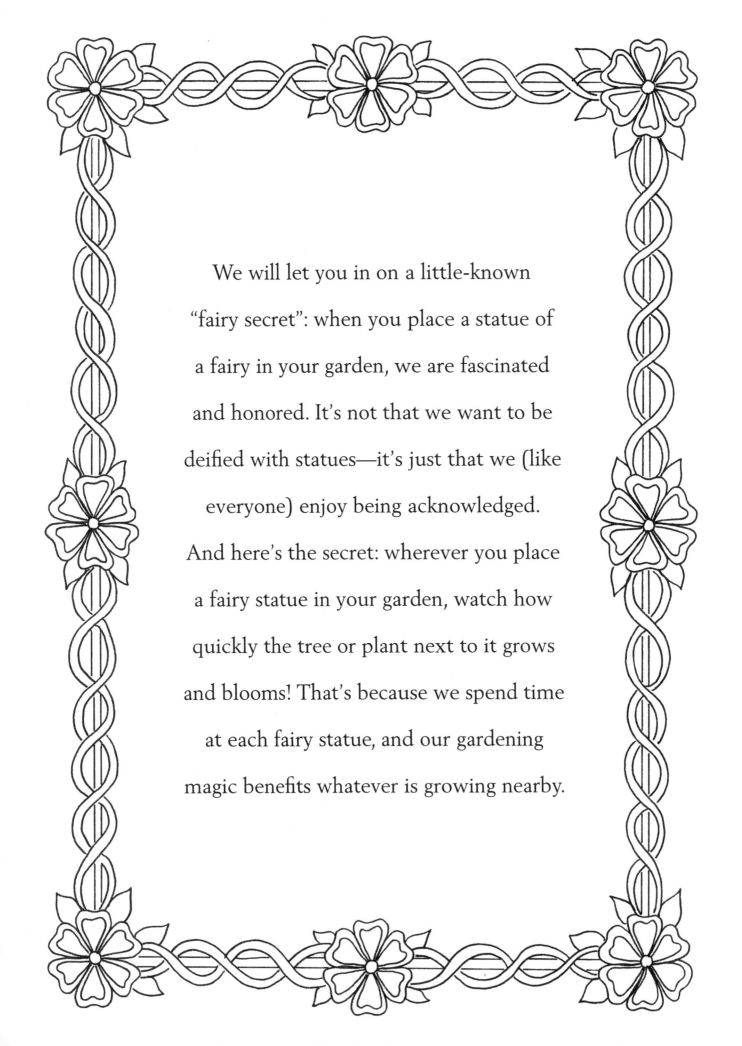

We will let you in on a little-known "fairy secret": when you place a statue of a fairy in your garden, we are fascinated and honored. It's not that we want to be deified with statues—it's just that we (like everyone) enjoy being acknowledged. And here's the secret: wherever you place a fairy statue in your garden, watch how quickly the tree or plant next to it grows and blooms! That's because we spend time at each fairy statue, and our gardening magic benefits whatever is growing nearby.

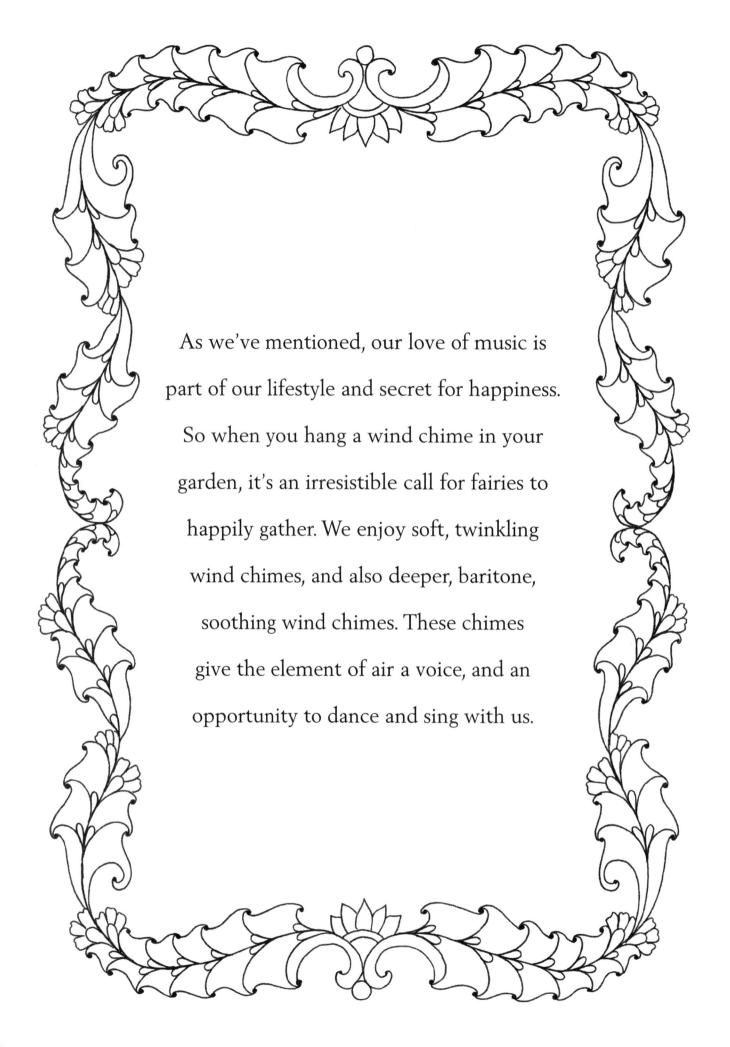

As we've mentioned, our love of music is part of our lifestyle and secret for happiness. So when you hang a wind chime in your garden, it's an irresistible call for fairies to happily gather. We enjoy soft, twinkling wind chimes, and also deeper, baritone, soothing wind chimes. These chimes give the element of air a voice, and an opportunity to dance and sing with us.

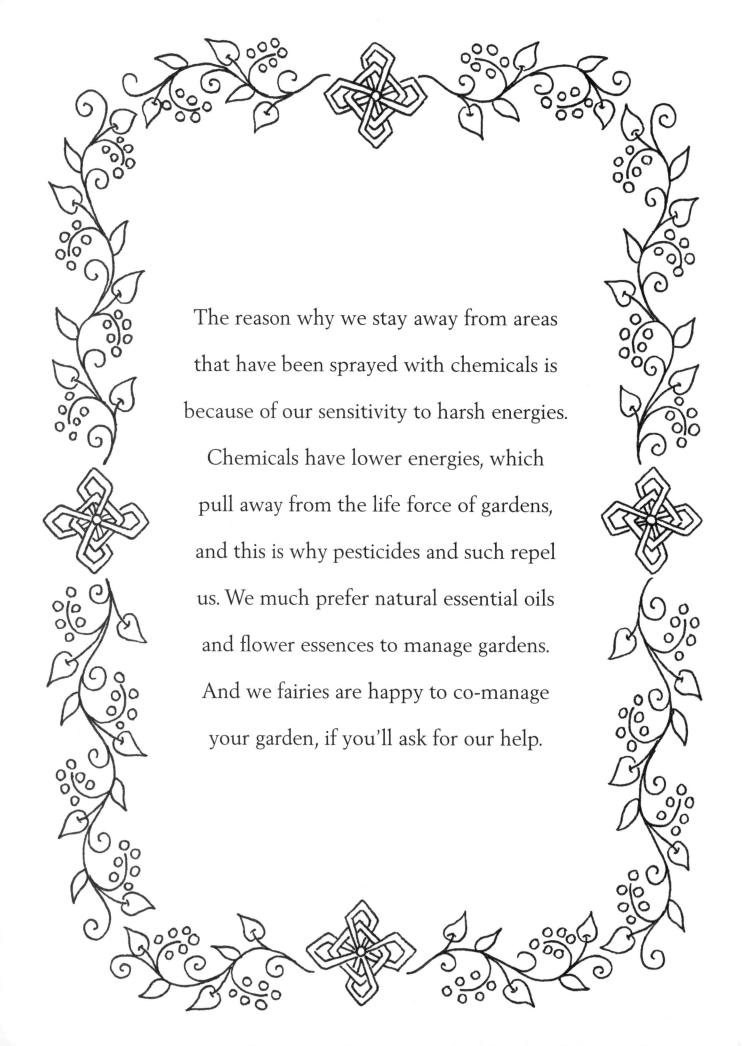

The reason why we stay away from areas
that have been sprayed with chemicals is
because of our sensitivity to harsh energies.
Chemicals have lower energies, which
pull away from the life force of gardens,
and this is why pesticides and such repel
us. We much prefer natural essential oils
and flower essences to manage gardens.
And we fairies are happy to co-manage
your garden, if you'll ask for our help.

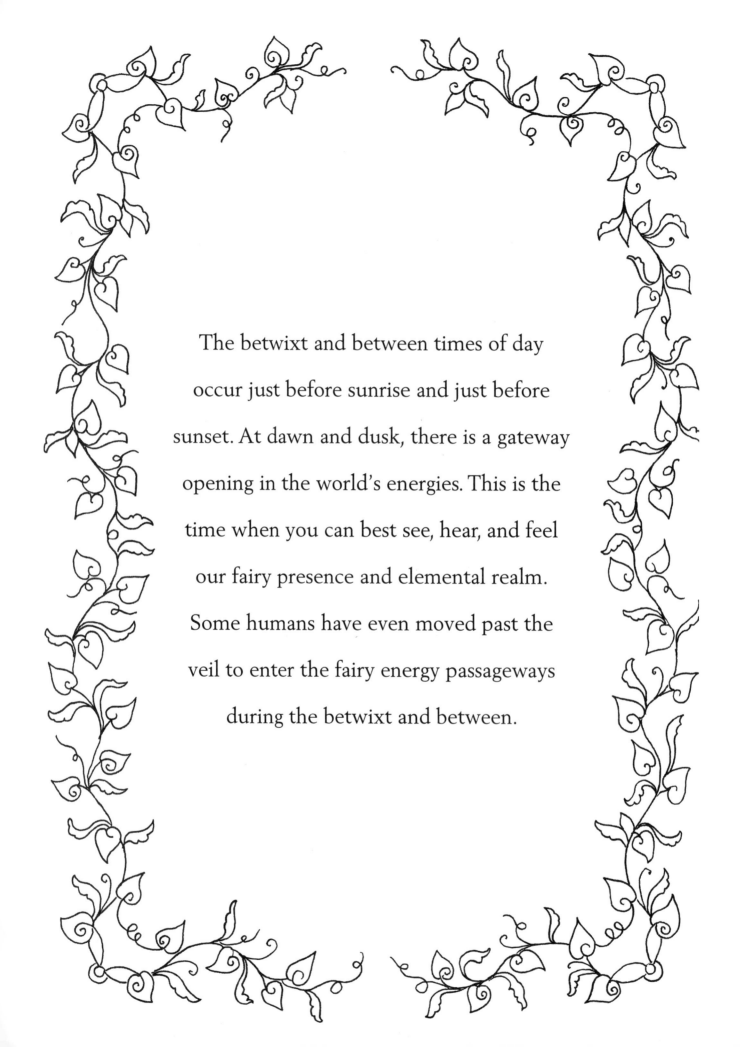

The betwixt and between times of day occur just before sunrise and just before sunset. At dawn and dusk, there is a gateway opening in the world's energies. This is the time when you can best see, hear, and feel our fairy presence and elemental realm. Some humans have even moved past the veil to enter the fairy energy passageways during the betwixt and between.

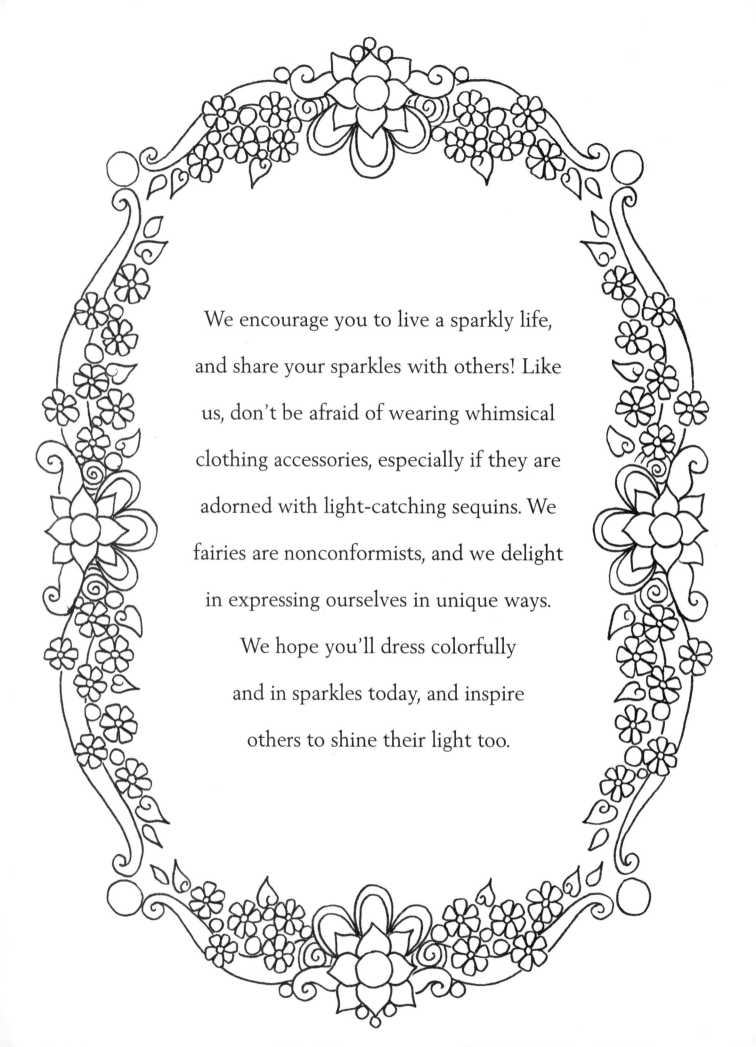

We encourage you to live a sparkly life, and share your sparkles with others! Like us, don't be afraid of wearing whimsical clothing accessories, especially if they are adorned with light-catching sequins. We fairies are nonconformists, and we delight in expressing ourselves in unique ways. We hope you'll dress colorfully and in sparkles today, and inspire others to shine their light too.

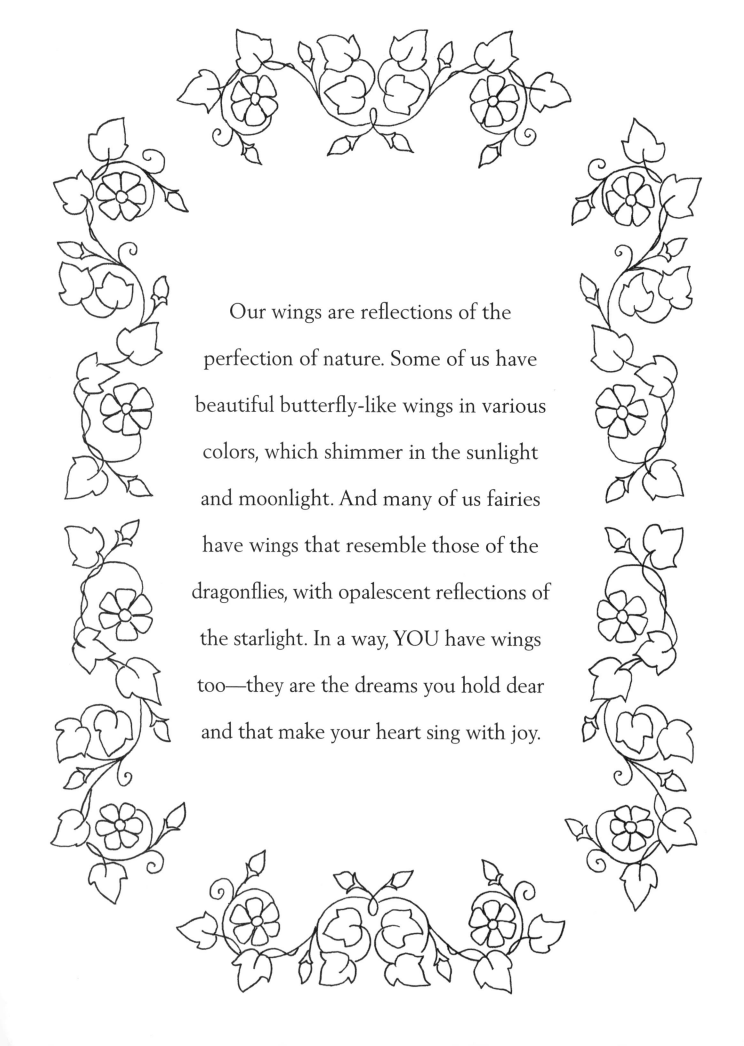

Our wings are reflections of the
perfection of nature. Some of us have
beautiful butterfly-like wings in various
colors, which shimmer in the sunlight
and moonlight. And many of us fairies
have wings that resemble those of the
dragonflies, with opalescent reflections of
the starlight. In a way, YOU have wings
too—they are the dreams you hold dear
and that make your heart sing with joy.

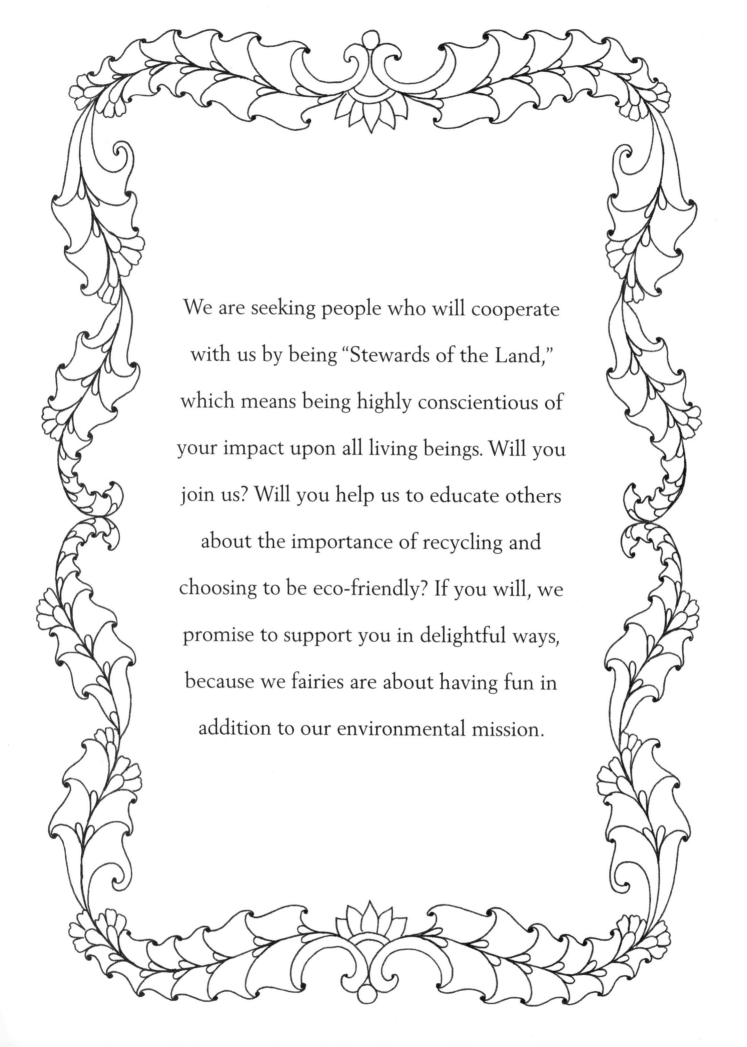

We are seeking people who will cooperate with us by being "Stewards of the Land," which means being highly conscientious of your impact upon all living beings. Will you join us? Will you help us to educate others about the importance of recycling and choosing to be eco-friendly? If you will, we promise to support you in delightful ways, because we fairies are about having fun in addition to our environmental mission.

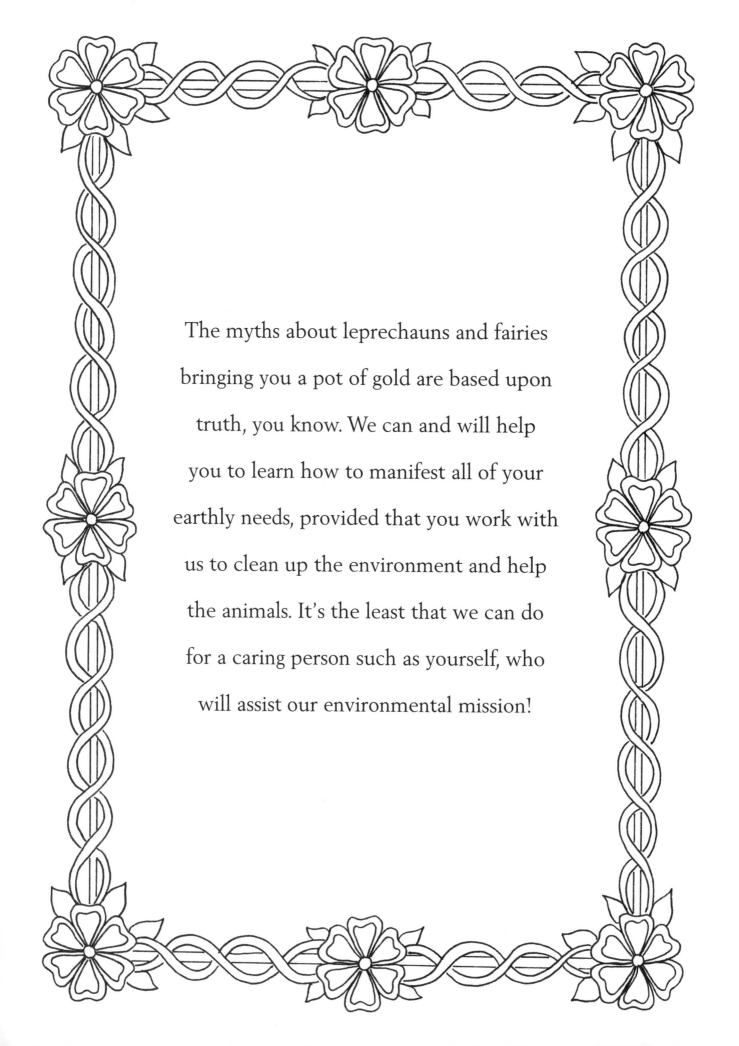

The myths about leprechauns and fairies bringing you a pot of gold are based upon truth, you know. We can and will help you to learn how to manifest all of your earthly needs, provided that you work with us to clean up the environment and help the animals. It's the least that we can do for a caring person such as yourself, who will assist our environmental mission!

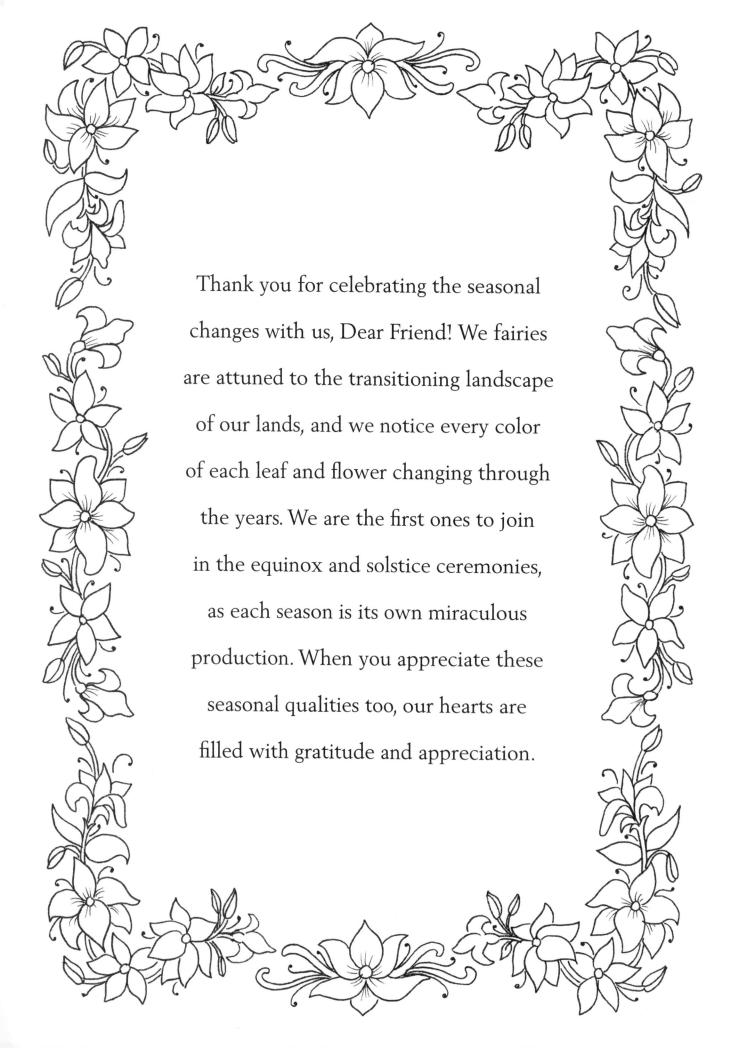

Thank you for celebrating the seasonal changes with us, Dear Friend! We fairies are attuned to the transitioning landscape of our lands, and we notice every color of each leaf and flower changing through the years. We are the first ones to join in the equinox and solstice ceremonies, as each season is its own miraculous production. When you appreciate these seasonal qualities too, our hearts are filled with gratitude and appreciation.

Moonlight is a nightly occurrence,

no matter what the phase of the moon.

We fairies hold nightly parties beneath

the moon. And while we prefer the big,

full moons, we also revel in the mysterious

unveiling that the dark moon offers to us

all. We invite you to take "moon baths"

with us by standing beneath the moon

and holding the intention of releasing

all that is unwanted and unneeded.

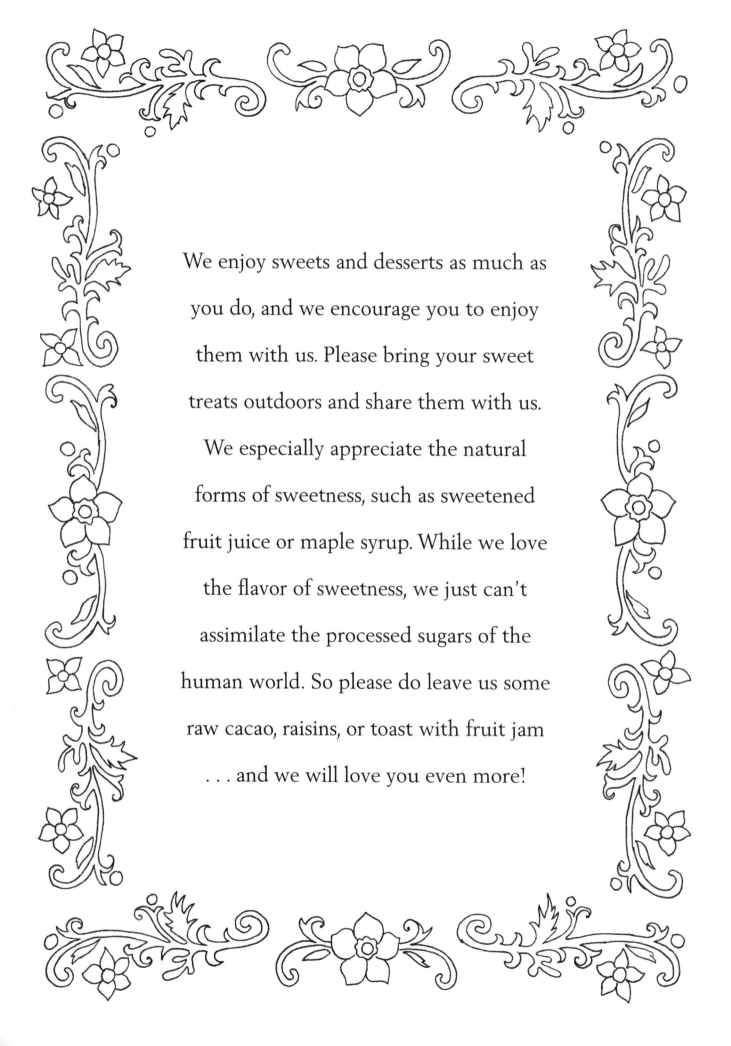

We enjoy sweets and desserts as much as you do, and we encourage you to enjoy them with us. Please bring your sweet treats outdoors and share them with us. We especially appreciate the natural forms of sweetness, such as sweetened fruit juice or maple syrup. While we love the flavor of sweetness, we just can't assimilate the processed sugars of the human world. So please do leave us some raw cacao, raisins, or toast with fruit jam . . . and we will love you even more!

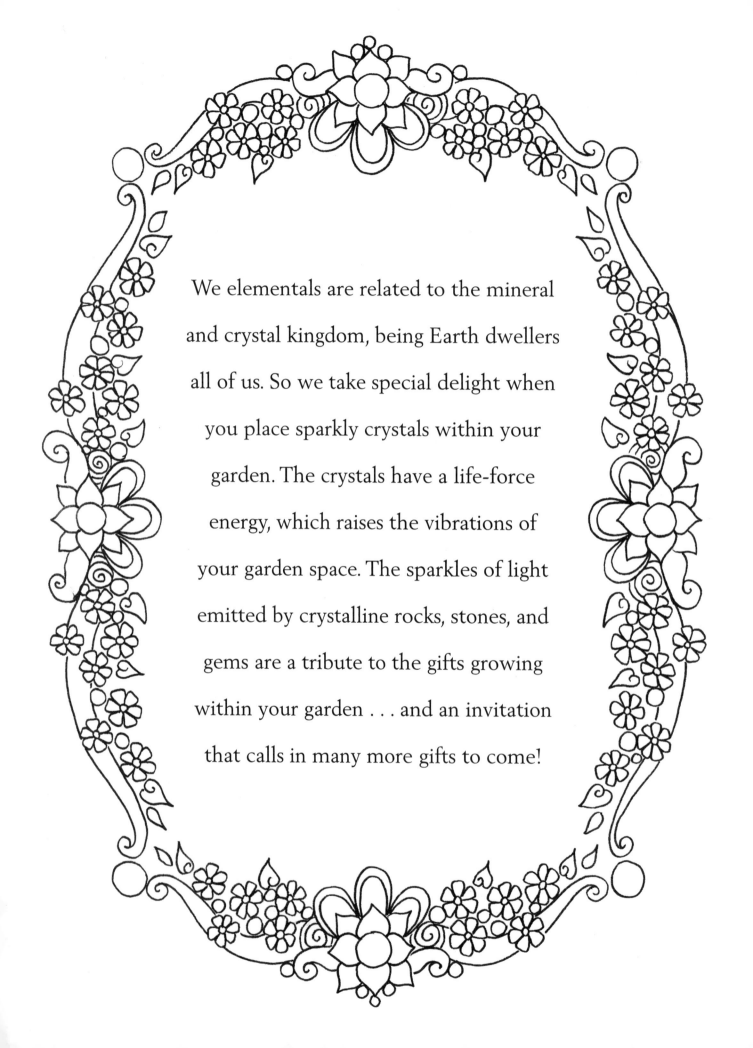

We elementals are related to the mineral and crystal kingdom, being Earth dwellers all of us. So we take special delight when you place sparkly crystals within your garden. The crystals have a life-force energy, which raises the vibrations of your garden space. The sparkles of light emitted by crystalline rocks, stones, and gems are a tribute to the gifts growing within your garden . . . and an invitation that calls in many more gifts to come!

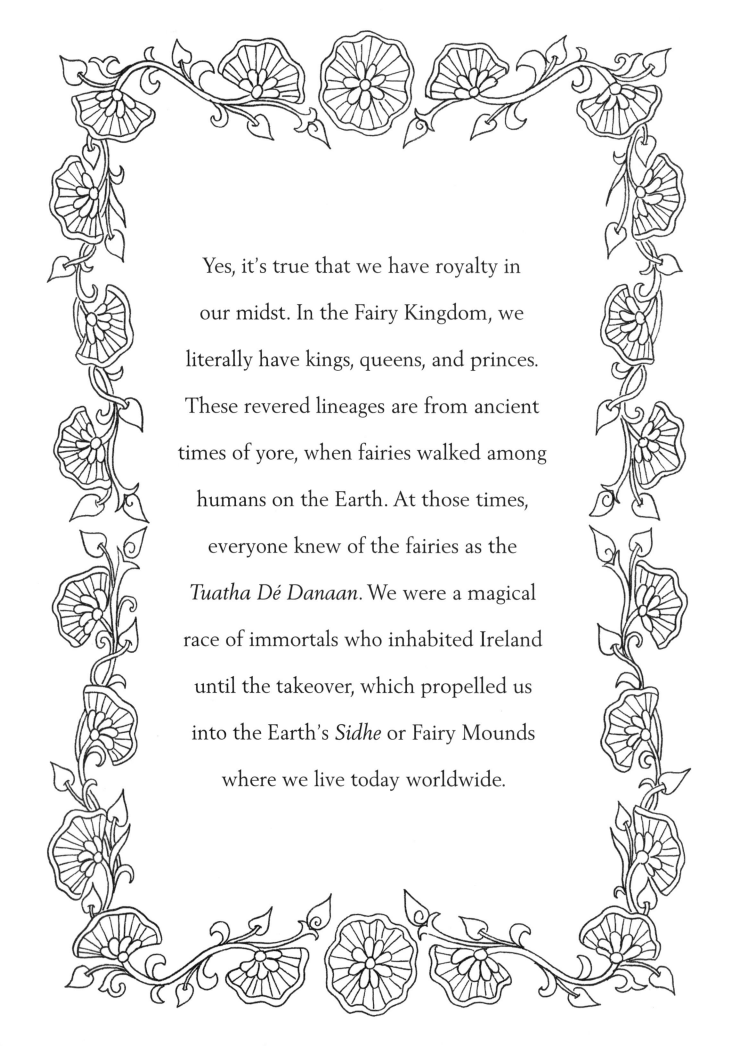

Yes, it's true that we have royalty in our midst. In the Fairy Kingdom, we literally have kings, queens, and princes. These revered lineages are from ancient times of yore, when fairies walked among humans on the Earth. At those times, everyone knew of the fairies as the *Tuatha Dé Danaan.* We were a magical race of immortals who inhabited Ireland until the takeover, which propelled us into the Earth's *Sidhe* or Fairy Mounds where we live today worldwide.

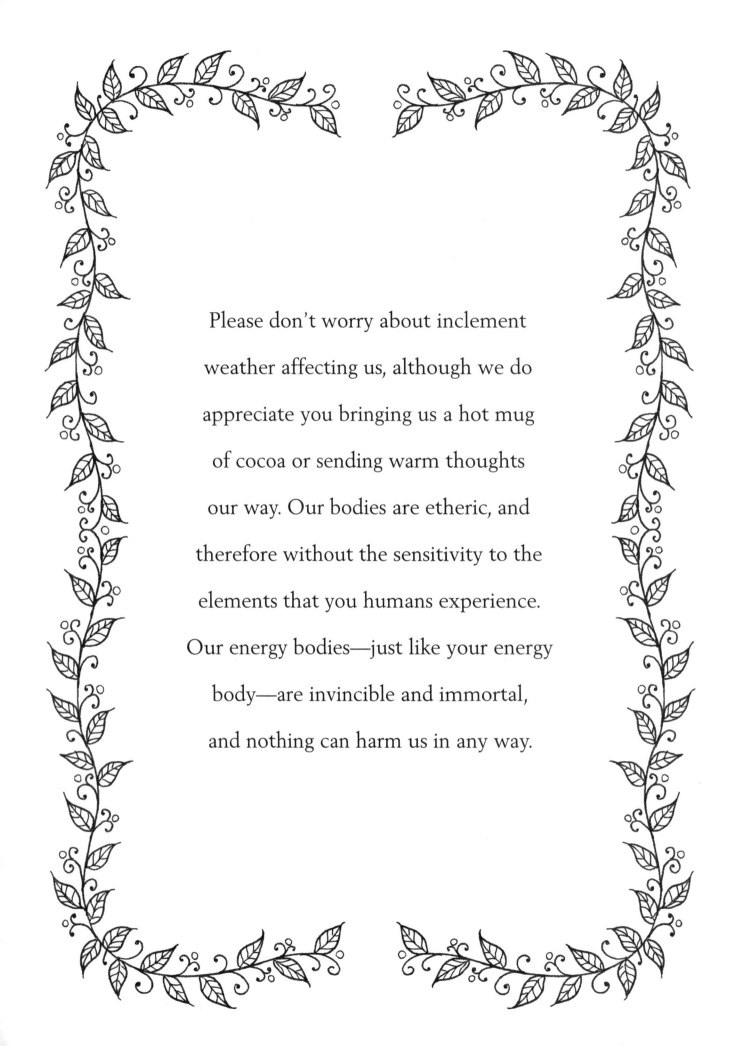

Please don't worry about inclement
weather affecting us, although we do
appreciate you bringing us a hot mug
of cocoa or sending warm thoughts
our way. Our bodies are etheric, and
therefore without the sensitivity to the
elements that you humans experience.
Our energy bodies—just like your energy
body—are invincible and immortal,
and nothing can harm us in any way.

We do appreciate your love and warm
hospitality, as we also love you too!
We are here on Earth for a mission, and
that's to protect her fragile balance. When
you acknowledge us, we feel loved and
appreciated. When you give us gifts of
sweets, sparkles, and little fairy homes
or rings, we flutter with excitement.
For when we find a person who treats
us like a friend, we go out of our way
to be the best friend ever in return.

## About the Author

Doreen Virtue holds B.A., M.A., and Ph.D. degrees in counseling psychology. She's the author of more than 50 books and oracle card decks dealing with spiritual topics. Best known for her work with the angels, Doreen is frequently called "The Angel Lady."

A lifelong activist and a vegan since 1996, Doreen is involved in charities and movements that support a healthy environment, fair treatment of animals, clean air and water, and organic non-GMO food for all.

Doreen has appeared on *Oprah*, CNN, and other television and radio programs, and writes the weekly column "Your Guardian Angel" for *Woman's World* magazine. Her products are available in most languages worldwide, on Kindle and other e-book platforms, and as iTunes apps. She also has a live weekly radio show on HayHouseRadio.com.

**www.angeltherapy.com**

## About the Illustrator

Norma J. Burnell, certified Zentangle® teacher, is an accomplished artist and has been involved in the arts all of her life. She is a contributing author to *The Art of Zentangle* and to *The Art of Fashion Tangling*.

After discovering the art of Zentangle, Norma began incorporating "tangles" into her own fantasy art and Fairy-Tangles™ was born. Many of her Fairy-Tangles drawings are now sold as rubber stamps for card making and other crafts, and her originals have been sold to collectors around the world.

Norma currently works for a small company creating websites and graphic design. She also teaches various art classes and continues to develop her own art. Her lifelong dream is to continue being an artist and to share her art with others.

**www.fairy-tangles.com**

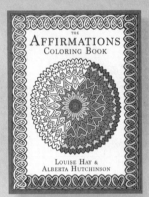

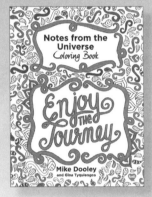